KNOW YOUR
MEDICAL RIGHTS

BATTLE MANUALS FOR FREEDOM
BOOK 1

A. LE ROY

UNPARAGONED

BATTLE MANUALS FOR FREEDOM

BY A. LEROY

Book 1: *Know Your Medical Rights*

Book 2: *Know Your Lawful Rights*

Book 3: *Know Your Financial Rights*

https://Geni.us/Rights

Battle Manuals for Freedom by Abdiel LeRoy

Weapons of Law and Constitutional Armour for the Battles Ahead

BATTLE MANUALS FOR FREEDOM
D. ASKROY

Book 1: Know Your Consumer Rights

Book 2: Know Your Lawful Rights

Book 3: Know Your Financial Rights

BattleManualsForRights

CONTENTS

Introduction   ix

PART I
OUR CORE FOUNDATION

BRIDGING POLITICAL DIVIDES   3
BRIDGING MEDICAL DIVIDES   4

PART II
OUR CONSTITUTIONAL
FOUNDATION

CONSTITUTIONS OVERRULE
LEGISLATION   17

PART III
OUR COMMON-LAW FOUNDATION

COMMON LAW OVERRULES
LEGISLATION   29
Caught courts   37

COMMON-LAW POLICING   40

PART IV
OUR MEDICAL FOUNDATION

MEDICAL EXPERIMENTATION   49

MEDICAL TREATMENT   57
Uninformed consent   61
Children   64

MEDICAL TESTING   73
MEDICAL CONFIDENTIALITY   75

MEDICAL DISCRIMINATION   80
Continental drift   85

MEDICAL INCARCERATION   88
Travel Rights   92
Community Rights   94

PART V

THE ERA OF FALSE PROPHETS

THE FATHER OF LIES   103
Exaggerating threat   105
Hiding injection injuries   106
Pfizer's Abortion Jab   111

PRINCE OF THE AIR (WAVES)   115
ACCUSER OF THE RIGHTEOUS   117
A REIGN OF FEAR   123
THE LOVE OF MONEY   130
THE RISE AND FALL OF IDOLATRY   134
THE NEPHILIM DESCENDANTS   142

PART VI

A NEW EARTH

THE TIME OF TRUE PROPHETS   149
CASTING OUT FEAR   154

PART VII

OUR BRUSH WITH
FALSE AUTHORITY

ASSERTING AND UPHOLDING
OUR RIGHTS   169

INTERACTING WITH POLICE   174
Protests   176
Filming the police   177
Searches   178

INTERACTING WITH YOUR EMPLOYER   180
INTERACTING WITH YOUR
CHILD'S SCHOOL   183
MASKS   184
JUDICIAL REVIEW IN BRITAIN   187
FINES   188

PART VIII

OUR OVERTHROW OF
FALSE AUTHORITY

THE NEW NAZI HUNTERS   193
CONCLUSION   199
CODA   211

Introduction to Know Your Lawful Rights   219
From the Author   239

BOOKS BY A. LEROY (ABDIEL LEROY)

NON-FICTION   245
POETRY COLLECTIONS   250
EPIC POETRY   254
(Fiction in Verse)
FICTION   256

APPENDIXES

APPENDIX I   261
A Handy Guide to Constitutional and Rights Protections
APPENDIX II   286
The 'Medical-Freedom Movement' Could Get Us All Killed!
APPENDIX III   293
To Brothers and Sisters in 'Healthcare'
APPENDIX IV   296
To Arbiters of 'Religious Exemption'
APPENDIX V   299
To Brothers and Sisters in Policing
APPENDIX VI   302
Letter to U.K. 'Ministry of Justice' Regarding Proposed Desecration of U.K. Human Rights Act
APPENDIX VII   304
Declaration to Riot Police
APPENDIX VIII   306
Other Resources
APPENDIX IX   315
Repairing Injection Damage

Notes   319

INTRODUCTION

I was brought up by my mother on the Bible, and she told me something that I've never forgotten. She said the stories in the Bible are stories about the conflict between the kings who have power and the prophets who preach righteousness, and she taught me to support the prophets and not the kings.

— TONY BENN, FORMER BRITISH
MEMBER OF PARLIAMENT, MAR. 10, 2006

I am writing this book because I have to, and because I know a confrontation is coming. No longer can I maintain the old uneasy coexistence with false authority, lamenting its folly and fraud, deploring its ignorance, and ridiculing its absurdities, but all from a safe distance. No, I am on a collision course with false authority, and I dare say you are too. We need to be prepared.

I have lived and worked on four continents, swum in

three oceans, heard innumerable foreign tongues, and observed the infinite variety of our species, but now the autocrats, bureaucrats, and technocrats, in their little, brief, and fear-fueled authority, would have us undergo invasive medical procedures, and hand over private medical information once held sacred, just to travel, to go about our lives, and even to make a living.

Time was when I could grudgingly accept mask requirements in the early days, frown at destructive lockdowns, and ignore voicemails and messages to my mobile phone from Britain's National Health Service (NHS). And I could largely dismiss the barrage of fearmongering propaganda that managed to circumvent my longstanding aversion to mainstream media. But when governments started threatening and penalizing bodily autonomy, a line was crossed.

I know in my heart that these measures are an atrocity, and my spirit rebels against them, but just having that instinct is not enough now. **WHAT ARE MY RIGHTS?!** I'm going to need more than mere disgust if I am to overrule the fearmongering autocrats who will exploit any emergency to unleash tyranny. I'm going to need constitutional armour and weapons of law, and I'm going to need them quickly. And when I have them, I will share them with those who may benefit.

Hence this book, a garment of protection for the 'COVID' era and an antidote to fear. I don't mean fear of a disease, but of the reactions—or rather overreactions —to it. Though I once entertained some background anxiety about a supposed virus, it's as nothing compared to the deep dread I've experienced about a totalitarian state emerging such as Orwell set out in *1984*.

I have also come to realize that even *that* kind of fear is being stoked by governments. At the outset, they wanted us to fear COVID, but after that got them only so far, now they want us to fear them, so that we won't make trouble.

For that type of fear, I recall the predicament of Moses' Israelites lately released from slavery in Egypt, as recounted in the Bible book of *Exodus*. Imagine their terror to realize Pharaoh's entire army was bearing down on them as they approached the Red Sea (14:10). But Moses told them not to fear, to stand firm, for they would see the Lord's deliverance. And they did, when the Red Sea drowned Pharaoh and his horde (14:28).

Therefore, no matter how bad things appear to get, the final chapter of our story sees the demise of slavery on Earth, including wage slavery, debt slavery, tax slavery, prison slavery, sex slavery, digital slavery and, of course, medical slavery, along with the deaths of tyrant politicians, bureaucrats, and corporate profiteers when, like a mighty river, Justice returns.

The 'vaccines', too, have an obvious allegory in the *Exodus* story. When Moses and his brother Aaron come to Pharaoh's court and issue their demands, Aaron demonstrates the power of God by turning his staff into a snake. Pharaoh's conjurors imitate the act, but Aaron's snake eats their snakes (7:12). Similarly, the fanged creatures of Pfizer, Moderna, AstraZeneca, and Johnson &

Johnson are no match for the lethal bite of truth-tellers, prophets, and whistleblowers today.

Also destined for destruction are the media organizations who have mouthpieced for the medical-industrial complex. I shudder to recall the *Daily Telegraph* front-page headline of July 21, 2021: "Freedom for double jabbed as UK opens to world." As if freedom can be granted or withheld at official whim, as if medical status were the qualification to receive it. No, we are born with it, and trying to take it away from us is blasphemy, no less an atrocity than the 'intercision' of Philip Pullman's novel, *The Golden Compass*, where the authorities cut children away from their 'daemon' animals, equivalent to extracting their souls.

The *Telegraph* also predicted, in a July-2021 article, "The unvaccinated will be shut out of normal life, progressively demonised, and stripped of civil rights..." And other mainstream outlets salivated at the prospect. As 2021 drew to a close, a quick glance at recent headlines showed an almost desperate eagerness to foment hatred against a vilified underclass. "The unvaccinated are putting us all at risk," squealed *The Times* of London. "I'm Furious at the Unvaccinated," howled *The New York Times*. "It is only a matter of time before we turn on the unvaccinated," thundered *The Guardian*.

Just like the cultist politicians and bureaucrats, these media mercenaries for Big Pharma know not what they say or what they do. Nor do they know or care that international statute defines persecution against an identifiable group as a Crime Against Humanity. Have all these puppets learned nothing from history and the madness of going after a targeted minority? Has it taken but a few generations to overturn what our ancestors fought and died for? Have these people lost their minds? I think they have!

We of prophetic calling have our work cut out for us, not just seeing, or warning against, future scenarios, as exemplified by Orwell, but in describing the present. That means observing the obvious and stating the obvious when populations are conditioned to overlook the obvious, to deny it to themselves and, even if they do see it, to keep quiet about it. As famed whistleblower Edward Snowden observes, "Everywhere we look, from Afghanistan to economics, from pandemic to pervasive surveillance, the obvious has been made unspeakable."[1]

And it is obvious that the medical-industrial complex, taking its playbook from the *military*-industrial complex, grooms politicians to do its bidding. It also likens the COVID response to war, reflecting the imperial and imperious mindset infecting our politics, with words like battle, beat, conquer, crush, defeat, eliminate, enemy, fight, front lines, victory, etc.

There *is* a war being waged, certainly, but of a very different kind, as encapsulated by the apostle Paul in the New Testament: "For our struggle is not against flesh and blood, but against the rulers, against the authorities, against the powers of this dark world and against the spiritual forces of evil in the heavenly realms" (*Ephesians* 6:12).

And those spiritual forces are especially murderous

towards children, recalling the ancient abomination of child sacrifice to Molech.

> "The Lord said to Moses, 'Say to the Israelites: Any Israelite or any foreigner residing in Israel who sacrifices any of his children to Molek is to be put to death. The members of the community are to stone him. I myself will set my face against him and will cut him off from his people; for by sacrificing his children to Molek, he has defiled my sanctuary and profaned my holy name. If the members of the community close their eyes when that man sacrifices one of his children to Molek and if they fail to put him to death, I myself will set my face against him and his family and will cut them off from their people, together with all who follow him in prostituting themselves to Molek.' "
>
> — *LEVITICUS* 20:1-5

Of course, fraud, corruption, and greed have always greased the wheels of government, but now we observe something far deadlier, a medical cult that demands human sacrifice, a religion of death, served by a conclave of tyrant priests in positions of false authority. The more they kill, the higher they rise in their infernal ranks.

I wish the figureheads of our so-called 'medical-freedom movement' would see this. I wish they would realize that the pharmaceutical complex is not so much counting the dollars as it is counting the bodies.

I came to this realization when hearing renowned

liver-health specialist and author, Dr. Burt Berkson, tell Dr. Jonathan Landsman in an interview, "At many medical schools, in many university hospitals, they give an award every month to the doctor who has the most deaths on his service, and they have a party, and it's called a 'Black Crow Award'."

Is that what this is all about? Are we in the middle of a global Black Crow Award now, in which medical professionals and hospitals and so-called health ministers are competing to see who can add the most corpses to the pile of medical waste? Or have they been assigned kill quotas?

That medical-freedom leaders overlook this deeper motivation is disappointing, but many more errors, and possibly fatal ones, they make besides. Most dangerous of all is to base their opposition to medical compulsion not on the solid ground that it is eternally unlawful, but on the shifting sands of data and statistics.

For example, they argue that this disease, or that variant, is too mild to warrant medical enforcements. Meaning what? That if some more deadly disease were conjured, they'd be fine with coercion?

That is boggy ground to build on, to paraphrase Herman Melville. Of course, autocrats are always ready to unleash another emergency which they will cite as pretext for more crackdowns and despotic legislation which they falsely call 'law'.

We also hear the medical-freedom caucus arguing certain measures should not be mandated because they are unproven, unsafe, or ineffective. Or because natural immunity is a thing, or asymptomatic spread is not a thing.

Fools! There is no 'because'! No medical measure can ever be compulsory—period, end of—whatever claims are asserted for its safety or effectiveness.

And here's the stupidest slogan of all. "Where there is risk, there must be choice." Meaning what? That if some medical treatment is concocted, and safety claimed for it, then choice can be taken away?

Misguided, too, are requests for 'exemption' from medical enforcement. These buy into a fiction that government has authority to demand anything from us in the first place. It doesn't. Quite the opposite. We have authority over government, and the word "No" is, always has been, and always will be, exemption enough.

Exemption requests also desecrate medical confidentiality when your medical status is nobody else's business in the first place. It is not the government's business, not your employer's business, not a travel company's business, and not your neighbour's business. Respect confidentiality, and your medical status can never be weaponized against you.

Our resolve against medical dictatorship, therefore, can never rest on competing views about today's data and circumstances but must instead be anchored in **CONSTITUTIONALITY**. Blind to emergency by design, constitutional principles are eternal and can't be swayed by the shifting currents of perception and statistics. They don't give a fuck about conditions on the ground, and nor should they. No, these times call us to be **CONSTITUTIONAL EXTREMISTS**.

Lawyers, too, need to grasp this. They whimper about not being able to go after pharmaceutical companies, doctors, hospitals, or regulators because of 'legal immunity'. Servile creatures, I rebuke your compliance with tyrant fictions spun to enslave Mankind. The Acts and statutes you cite—and stop calling them laws—these licences to kill, are nothing more than corporate contracts that one party has drafted, one party has signed, and one party has negotiated with itself. Yet that party thinks to impose those contracts on another party, us, to codify enslavement, murder, extortion, destruction, and theft, and then to pardon itself of the crimes. As we shall see, in the coming section on Common Law, these instruments are powerless without our signature, and not worth the air they're written on.

Imagine you were a business owner seeking to procure goods from a supplier, but that supplier gets to write the contract without your review, and that contract binds you as soon as the ink is dry without your knowledge, signature, or consent. You'd tell them to get lost, wouldn't you? Yet that is the bargain that governments and their corporate conspirators think to impose, and before which our conditioned cadre of cringing lawyers think to kneel. When will you stop enthroning legislation over Justice?!

One rare exception to this tendency is British human-rights lawyer, Anna de Buisseret. Interviewed in London's

Parliament Square during a Medical Freedom March of Oct. 30, 2021, she advises:

> "Learn what your fundamental, inalienable human rights are. Anyone who can access Google, you google the Universal Declaration of Human Rights, read it, read the European Convention on Human Rights, read the U.K. Human Rights Act, read the International Covenant on Social and Political and Economic Rights. Those rights are all there. It's all there in the law. The reason this is happening is because people don't know the law, so they don't know how to uphold it and assert it."

I applaud the spirit of her words, though that's an awful lot of homework for your average freedom-loving reader to do, especially if you add in the 170-page Notice of Liability, prepared by de Buisseret and her allies in Lawyers for Liberty, to serve against skin piercers and their accomplices. But I *have* done the homework and distilled into this book the key language that empowers us.

The good news is that none of this is complicated. It doesn't require a law degree, nor a thorough grounding in Latin. The beauty of these universal principles lies in their plain-English simplicity and, like the proverbial mustard seed of faith that overthrows mountains,[2] our little understanding in this arena goes a long way in vaulting the pronouncements of foolish and fearful men. A layman's expertise will do, and a layman's analysis can provide it, which is why I am as qualified as anyone else to do so here.

Brothers and sisters, it is time to release from their glass cabinets the dusty scrolls of our Rights declarations. We reclaim the keys that unleash them and, like the true prophets of old, proclaim them again to break the spells and incantations of false priests now roaming the Earth.

Our Rights, being inalienable, or unalienable if you prefer, were never granted by a gift of government nor rescinded by a denial of government. In the words of John K. Webster, creator of the documentary *Strawman*,

"GOVERNMENT IS A CREATION OF MAN, AND A CREATION OF MAN CAN NEVER BE ABOVE MAN."

So, if governments will not hear or heed the simple and time-honoured constitutional principles they are sworn to uphold, then each of us must acquire at least a little expertise in this area.

Nor will I pin my hopes on a political party or candidate to produce a regime a little less vindictive than the last. Love for our Rights straddles the old divides where antagonists are merely co-conspirators in bipartisan acts of theft. As Martin Luther wrote of the papists and anabaptists in 1531, "These foxes are tied together by the tails, even though their heads look in opposite directions. While they outwardly profess to be great enemies, inwardly they think, teach, and defend one and the same thing." Once we realize this, and expose the unholy alliances against our core values, whether by Democrat with Republican, Tory with Labour, or by any other duopoly or coalition, we can be rid of this corrupt political theatre altogether.

We are in a Declaration-of-Independence moment when an entire *form* of government, not just a faction *within* government, is destroying Life, Liberty, and the Pursuit of Happiness. It is therefore our duty now to abolish *this* form of government, maybe even the entire *idea* of government (which means 'mind control'). We are not fighting in a horizontal plane of 'Left' versus 'Right', but in the vertical plane of Life over Death, Creation over Destruction, Love over Fear.

That is a spiritual battle, the battle for which this book is conceived. May this declaration in words empower us to "suit the action to the word, the word to the action"[3] as we hear and heed the rallying call from the Captain of our souls, he whose Word "is alive and active, and sharper than any double-edged sword" (*Hebrews* 4:12).

Allied with that weapon is our sword of constitutional truth. It pulses with Heaven's call for Justice, imparts courage to those who wield it, and thirsts for the blood of today's cabal of thieves and murderers, whether in government, media, or any other organization. Let us pursue them with the kind of fury that Elijah wielded in slaughtering the false prophets of Baal on Mount Carmel (*1 Kings* 18:40). For, as Dave Mason writes in his masterful *Age of Prophecy* novels,[4] set in the time of Elijah,

"Those who show mercy to the cruel, bring cruelty upon the merciful."

For those of us contemplating our first run-in with would-be enforcers such as police, the task ahead may appear daunting, but here I share the vital information we will need if menaced by state or corporation, and if you have a paperback version, I hope it shall become marked up with your highlights and scribblings.

Our quest may seem to present impossible odds. Well, you would have said the same of Moses and Aaron going up against Pharaoh, his court, his paymasters, slave masters, chariots, and weaponry. But he who was in the prophets was greater than he who was in Pharaoh, and he who is in us now is greater than he who is in the autocrats, bureaucrats, technocrats, and 'psychocrats' of our age. And, oh yes, the 'philanthrocrats' too!

"Hold the line, stand your ground, uphold the rule of law, step into your sovereignty," De Buisseret urges in the closing moments of her Parliament-Square interview. "The law is all there to protect you, but you're not going to get protected unless you know what it is and you uphold it."

Therefore, we look to the eternal values of Mankind—values not swayed by political convenience and expediency, nor by profiteering motives, and that have *more* currency, not less, during times of emergency, whether that emergency is real or perceived or invented. So join me in the field, my friend. These times will make prophets of us all!

PART I

OUR CORE FOUNDATION

"This Jesus of Nazareth!" he cried. "This class-conscious workingman! This union carpenter! This agitator, lawbreaker, firebrand, anarchist!"

— UPTON SINCLAIR, *THE JUNGLE*

If you feel bewildered by the flurry of government decrees issued since COVID's arrival in 2020, you are not alone. A growing chorus of dissent, though largely ostracized from mainstream media, is finding expression through independent news and analysis, and the voices are finding each other. Refreshingly, this new unity is vaulting traditional political divides, which were ever an irrelevance to our higher values of life and love.

A new and more accurate divide has formed between we who love liberty and refuse to bow before medical and financial deities, and the tyrants who would order us to do so. Perhaps the most surprising development in these allegiances is that the advocates of unconstitutional enforcement include many on the so-called 'Left' who should know better, people who, until fear porn clouded their judgment, would see through mainstream-media spin and denounce corporations profiteering from crisis, call out legally sanctioned discrimination against the already disadvantaged, and rail against Big Pharma's capture of regulatory agencies.

Even the Green Party in America has aligned with Big Pharma's agenda, but its Black Caucus has not. In a statement published Dec. 13, 2021, the Caucus declares its alliance with the international Medical Freedom movement and denounces lockdowns, mandates, and passports as "the most vile, unconstitutional, immoral, unscientific, discriminatory and outright criminal policies ever enforced upon the population and go against everything the Green Party stands for under Social Justice."

BRIDGING POLITICAL DIVIDES

Allow me, then, to question any allegiance you may feel with one side or the other in any political duopoly. How many times have we poured our energies into supporting candidates who, once installed, have left us feeling disappointed at best and betrayed at worst? True voices of principle are excluded from the competition anyway, whether by manipulation within political parties, electoral fraud, or well-funded smear campaigns.

Do you really know what the terms 'left wing' or 'right wing' mean any more? Did you ever? And even if you did, is there anything to be gained in the horizontal plane of their contention? Consider the words of Colombian president, Gustavo Petro: "I no longer divide politics into left and right. I think that was a relatively logical way and a relatively realistic way to describe politics in the 20th century, but today, politics is divided between the politics of life and the politics of death."[1]

BRIDGING MEDICAL DIVIDES

Stop blaming your neighbor for the pain you are feeling… Don't be angry at a school-bus driver or a nurse or a teacher's aide. Be angry at the oligarchs. Don't let them turn us against each other, because that's what these mandates do.

— JIMMY DORE

Nor, crucially, is there a divide between vaccinated and unvaccinated. Quite the opposite. These divisions, along with various 'culture wars', are highly convenient to the pharaohs of this age who are quite happy to see us attack each other, rather than turn our collective attention towards them.

Therefore, we do not condemn the medical decision of another, much less gloat if that decision turns out to be misguided. We are all capable of making foolish, misguided, and ignorant choices, and those who suffer deserve our mercy and compassion, not condemnation. I've heard far too much "get-what-they-deserve" language on both sides and, in a chilling reminder of Death-Eater logic in the *Harry Potter* novels, reference to 'purebloods'. No, let us instead pledge to help, heal, serve, and comfort all who are afflicted, whether they made the same choice as us or not.

PART II

OUR CONSTITUTIONAL FOUNDATION

We know our Rights innately and instinctively, but they are enshrined in universal declarations to shield us from the predations of minister and monarch, bandit and bureaucrat, corporation and cult who would exploit, extort, and enslave others made in God's image if they could. These declarations, conventions, and constitutions are a sacred gift from our ancestors, from a chorus of witnesses[1] who now call on us to uphold their words, honour their legacy, and reassert our fundamental standing as sovereign men and women against the latest tide of blasphemy sweeping the Earth.

My general pattern in this book will be first to examine the bedrock principles on which our liberties rely, then to move from the universal and the eternal to international and European protections, followed by individual countries and institutions. All the emphases in the quotations are my own. First mentions of documents are in bold and linked (for those reading the electronic version of this book). Subsequent mentions are in bold and, where appropriate, in acronym form, such as **UDHR** for the ***Universal Declaration of Human Rights***.

Having lived most of my life in England and the united States, these are the nations I most readily discuss, but I am also paying closer attention to Australia and Canada now, where the totalitarian agenda is most alarmingly advanced. Later editions may go into more detail about more places, but time is of the essence, and I dare not wait another day to get this out. Still, wherever you live, the international protections apply.

And don't worry if you get lost trying to remember which declaration says what, and in what context. I've set out all the key protections in Appendix I, a handy guide to international and national Rights declarations, conventions, and codes. You will also find a link to download a PDF version for yourself.

In all, let us be motivated—and I say this as a reminder to myself too—not by fear but by love...

"Jesus replied, 'Thou shalt love the Lord thy God with all thy heart, and with all thy soul, and with all thy mind. This is the first and greatest commandment. And the second is like unto it, Thou shalt love thy neighbour as thyself.' "

— *MATTHEW* 22:37-39

This **Second Commandment** is also known as the **Golden Rule** or, as coined in the *Book of James*, **Royal Law**: "If indeed you keep the royal law according to the Scripture, 'You shall love your neighbour as yourself,' you are doing well" (*James* 2:8).

For example, is it love to impose my medical choice on another? Here, I yield the spotlight to Oscar Wilde:

> "A man is called selfish if he lives in the manner that seems to him most suitable for the full realisation of his own personality... But this is the way in which every one should live. Selfishness is not living as one wishes to live, it is asking others to live as one wishes to live. And unselfishness is letting other people's lives alone, not interfering with them. Selfishness always aims at creating around it an absolute uniformity of type. Unselfishness recognises infinite variety of type as a delightful thing, accepts it, acquiesces in it, enjoys it."

And we uphold the **First Commandment** as well—to love God—when we understand we are made in God's image (*Genesis* 1:26), that our body is a temple (*1 Corinthians* 3:16) and therefore sacred, and thus revere bodily autonomy for ourselves and others in all our representations of the divine.

But now, let's get into specifics of constitutional and Rights language. Once the **Golden Rule** is embraced, let us proceed to *Magna Carta*, our foundational constitutional text, drafted more than eight centuries ago as an antidote to King John, until recently the worst tyrant in English history. Learn this key statement...

"TO NO-ONE WILL WE SELL, TO NO-ONE WILL WE REFUSE OR DELAY, RIGHT OR JUSTICE."

— *MAGNA CARTA*, ARTICLE 40

By the light of this constitutional beacon, we need only ask of any edict, regulation, or stipulation, whether Rights were bought or sold to obtain it. In short, follow the money! Who paid whom to stifle our core Rights such as free speech, protest, privacy, legal redress, or even the Right to Life itself?

For example, what Rights were sold in 2020 when, even before injections started to roll out, the British government granted pre-emptive legal immunity to pharmaceutical companies, so that no-one could sue them for future harms?

I first became aware of this outrage to Justice in August 2020 when the British government published a so-called 'Consultation Document' titled *Changes to Human Medicine Regulations to Support the Rollout of COVID-19 Vaccines*.

That this was constructed on a foundation of lies was obvious from the opening sentence: "COVID-19 is the biggest threat this country has faced in peacetime history...." Glaringly overlooking the Black Death, the

Spanish Flu, and a succession of devastating plagues in-between. The very next paragraph was, if anything, even more fraudulent: "Effective COVID-19 vaccines will be the best way to deal with the pandemic." Pure speculation!

Yet on these fraudulent foundations, the Document insisted pharmaceutical manufacturers and others in the supply chain "cannot generally be sued in the civil courts for the consequences resulting from the use of an unlicensed product."

What objective observer would fail to infer the thumb of pharmaceutical companies on the scales of Justice and to conclude that industry lobbyists were dictating government policy? Of course, this was all conducted behind closed doors, but we get an insight into Big Pharma's manipulations from a February 2001 Bureau of Investigative Journalism report titled *Held to ransom: Pfizer demands governments gamble with state assets to secure vaccine deal.* The piece reveals Pfizer demanded countries in South America "put up sovereign assets, such as embassy buildings and military bases, as a guarantee... against any civil claims citizens might file if they experienced adverse effects after being inoculated."

The report also reveals, "Pfizer has been in talks with more than 100 countries and supranational organisations, and has supply agreements with nine countries in Latin America and the Caribbean: Chile, Colombia, Costa Rica, Dominican Republic, Ecuador, Mexico, Panama, Peru, and Uruguay. The terms of those deals are unknown."

In the U.S., the legal shields for Big Pharma went up

even earlier in 2020 when health secretary Alex Azar, a former pharmaceutical executive and lobbyist, invoked the Public Readiness and Emergency Preparedness (PREP) Act. This legislation, enacted in 2005, provides legal protection to U.S. companies making or distributing medical supplies like vaccines unless there is "willful misconduct." The products of Pfizer, Moderna, AstraZeneca, and Johnson & Johnson were also exempted from the National Vaccine Compensation Program.

Again, I invoke *Magna Carta* to decry this: "To no-one will we sell, to no-one will we refuse or delay, right or justice."

Consider too, what Rights were traded when Matt Hancock, the health minister initially presiding over Britain's 'pandemic' response, was giving COVID contracts to his friends, breaking his own protocols, and planning to "deploy" a new variant of COVID and to "frighten the pants [off] everyone with the new strain." Oh, and adulterously shagging a former lobbyist he had hired into his department. Such is the level of corruption in the British establishment, and it has been replicated throughout most of the world.

So, the **Royal Law** and *Magna Carta* are good anchors of principle for our constitutional understandings. I will also refer in this book to the *UDHR*, itself inspired by *Magna Carta*, and adopted by the United Nations in 1948. Its articles, as pointed out by Anna de Buisseret in her October 2021 interview, "are enshrined in multiple Human-Rights treaties and conventions, international, European, and U.K."

In 1966, the U.N. also ratified the *International Covenant on Economic, Social and Cultural Rights* (ICESCR) which hails "the inherent dignity of the human person" in its Preamble and begins its first Article, "All peoples have the right of self-determination" (Part I, Article 1, Para. 1).

In the same year, the U.N. took up the *International Covenant on Civil and Political Rights* (ICCPR) which states in Article 3, "Everyone has the right to life, liberty, and security of person." In 1984, this Covenant was cemented with the *Siracusa Principles* to ensure its protections would apply even in times of direst emergency:

> "No state party shall, **even in time of emergency threatening the life of the nation,** derogate from the Covenant's guarantees of the right to life; freedom from torture, cruel, inhuman or degrading treatment or punishment, and **from medical or scientific experimentation** without free consent; freedom from slavery or involuntary servitude; the right not to be imprisoned for contractual debt; the right not to be convicted or sentenced to a heavier penalty by virtue of retroactive criminal legislation; the right to recognition as a person before the law; and freedom of thought, conscience and religion. **These rights are not derogable under any conditions even for the asserted purpose of preserving the life of the nation**" (Para. 58).

"Not derogable" means your Rights cannot be set aside for any reason, cannot be diluted, cannot be impaired. They are non-negotiable. "A fundamental maxim of law is that you have sovereignty over your own mind and body," says de Buisseret...

> "Nobody gets to break that, not even in times of public emergency threatening the life of a nation. So the idea that a bunch of bureaucrats in 2020, 2021 get to come along and set aside our rule of law, claiming there's a public-health emergency, it's not legal, it's not lawful, it's not moral, it's not ethical."

Yes, as the *Siracusa Principles* spell out, constitutions are not plastic statements to be suspended or revoked at the whim of leaders and politicians, nor in times of emergency. On the contrary, knowing that power corrupts and will seize on any excuse to enlarge itself, they are there especially *for* times of emergency lest, reacting out of fear or panic, we find pretext to harm others. I therefore celebrate the *Principles'* use of the word 'asserted' in "the asserted purpose of preserving the life of the nation" above. The drafters knew political leaders would lie to the people about perceived dangers and claim their destructive measures were for our own good.

One such tyrant, of course, is Canadian prime minister, Justin Trudeau, who feels the unvaccinated are "taking up space." In an utter inversion of *Siracusa*, and for the first time in the nation's history, he seized so-called 'Emergency Powers' in early 2022 to persecute and terrorize truckers who opposed his Rights-crushing decrees. With the connivance of his vampiric finance minister, Chrystia Freeland, along with a supine finance industry and complicit police, he stole funds and even fuel from the movement, froze individual bank accounts of participants, and persecuted their donors and supporters. He cancelled insurance on truckers' vehicles, threatened to kidnap their children and kill their pets, dished out indiscriminate brutality at the hands of his Praetorian police force, and disappeared movement leaders who were snatched off street corners in the dark of night. Meanwhile, police in Canberra, Australia were directing radiation weapons against protestors, causing their skin to burn and blister.

Again, I say, be a **CONSTITUTIONAL EXTREMIST**! Constitutionality is the supreme authority, transcending the medical debates of the day. Even if a disease came along tomorrow to rival the Black Death and wiped out half the population, and even if there were some medical product proven 100% effective in preventing transmission and symptoms, and even if that product were completely guaranteed to be without side effects—and those, of course, are impossible ifs—any medical imposition would be a lawless atrocity, violating our sovereignty and transgressing bedrock constitutional protections as old as our species.

It is troubling to hear opponents of mandates base

their arguments on the low level, or absence of, emergency. No. Grow up in your constitutional understanding! Medical statistics are a dangerous distraction when, with awestruck wonder, we may look up and behold our true North Star of constitutionality.

CONSTITUTIONS OVERRULE LEGISLATION

The reason I talk about constitutions before addressing legislation, is that they are not the same, and often in direct opposition. Legislation, such as Acts or statutes, is typically drafted and/or applied to enforce tyranny, and then to shield the enforcers of that tyranny from any real justice.

Martin Luther King wrote in his famed *Letter From a Birmingham Jail* (1963) that "there are two types of laws: just and unjust" and that "one has a moral responsibility to disobey unjust laws. I would agree with St. Augustine that 'an unjust law is no law at all.' "

Agreed, except that King errs in calling legislation 'law'. As we shall see in the coming section on Common Law, legislative instruments are but corporate contracts written by one party who thinks to impose them unilaterally on another party, We the People, so...

STOP CALLING LEGISLATION 'LAW'!

The inherent opposition between legislation and constitutional Rights is explicitly recognized in the States in *United States Code* Title 18, Section 242, which specifies penalties for anyone who, "under color of any law, statute, ordinance, regulation, or custom, willfully subjects any person in any State, Territory, Commonwealth, Possession, or District to the deprivation of any rights, privileges, or immunities secured or protected by the Constitution or laws of the United States." If the violation results in bodily injury, the penalty can include ten years in prison. The *Code* even allows for life imprisonment or a death sentence in cases of kidnapping or sexual abuse.

History is littered with unjust legislation; indeed, it seems easier to find than just legislation. It includes Nazi Germany's legalization of forced sterilization in 1933, which followed similar measures in some American states. More recent examples of blatantly unconstitutional legislation include the *U.S. Military Commissions and Detainee Treatment Act* (2006) which immunized U.S. officials, and those who gave them orders, from prosecution for torturing prisoners, a clear breach of the **Eighth Amendment**'s prohibition of "cruel and unusual punishment."

Fast forward to December 2021, when the U.K. government "is taking away our liberties on an industrial scale," to quote journalist George Monbiot in a broadcast for Double Down News. At the time, two bills were making their way through Parliament: the *Police, Crime, Sentencing and Courts Bill*, which effectively bans protest and permits police to stop and search without suspicion; and the *Nationality and Borders Bill* which, in Clause 9, assumes the power to strip people of citizenship retrospectively and without warning. As Frances Webber, vice-chair of the Institute of Race Relations, observes, "It unapologetically flouts international human-rights obligations and basic norms of fairness."

Monbiot didn't get to the *Public Health (Control of Disease) Act* which contains new tyrannical impositions in Sections 45B and 45C that weren't in the original 1984 version. These dictate that "the appropriate Minister" may impose medical examination, detention, isolation, or quarantine of persons; seize, inspect, or destroy property; impose "disinfection" of persons; prohibit the entry or exit of persons or things; and require persons to answer questions about their health.

The minister may also, "in response to a threat to public health," make regulations "imposing duties on registered medical practitioners or other persons to record and notify cases or suspected cases of infection or contamination," require that children be kept away from school, prohibit events and gatherings, and dictate how dead bodies are handled and human remains disposed. And, oh yes, the Minister may impose any other "special restriction or requirement."

So, there you have it. Our politicians, officials, and bureaucrats want to be kings, not just kings but absolute monarchs, accountable to no-one, with the power to dictate every aspect of our lives, and deaths! In these two Sections alone, we see a presumptive carte-blanche to imprison any person indefinitely, seize any property, and "disinfect" anyone they choose on any public-health pretext. None of this is permissible under international law, as I have demonstrated or will demonstrate in this book. It is totalitarian madness, and we all know it.

We are living in a time of evil legislation—lawlessness cloaked in legislation—in which the terms 'legal' and 'illegal' no longer have any meaning and are utterly irrelevant to the truth in our hearts. Parliamentary rubber stamps add not one jot of legitimacy to tyrannical statutes. As the great author Robert Graves so colourfully put it, "Parliament may vote a turd to be a rose; but a turd it still remains!"[1]

And if Acts passed by legislatures are meaningless, how much more so the pronouncements and regulations of executive branches or government officials who never bothered with the troublesome business of parliamentary oversight, deliberation, or vote? As the website Laworfiction.com observes of such edicts in the U.K., "the dressing up of unenforceable policy guidance as enforceable rule of law is an issue of serious public concern."

Therefore, in the words of Rights defender, Dolores Cahill, in an August 2021 interview with Clive de Carle,...

"We need, in each of our countries, to ensure the rule of law exists, and the politicians and the media and the medical profession are not falsely told that just because there's a guideline, you can break the law, falsely told there is indemnity to an injection, which is entirely untrue."

That's not to say I will never call on Acts, statutes, or regulations to support our cause. Though they are not law, they are occasionally beneficial or protective, and therefore lawful. You and I are not bound by them, but the corporations *are* bound to comply with their own contracts. Therefore, we may run any legislation through a Rights sieve to separate the righteous from the unrighteous and cherry-pick from their documents when it serves us to do so.

Even within its own legal framework, the U.K. government has no standing for the emergency measures it has taken. As the Oxford Constitutional Law website explains, "There is no formal constitutional procedure for declaring a national state of emergency, but the *Civil Contingencies Act* (2004) is a statutory framework functionally equivalent thereto, the 'protection of health' being an emergency category under the Act. **It was not used.**" (Para. 11)

Why wasn't it used? Presumably because it cancels emergency regulations after seven days if not approved by each House of Parliament (Section 27, Para. 1(b)) and because it requires parliamentary renewal every 30 days (Section 26, Para. 1). Having fulfilled neither of these requirements, the British government is acting illegally.

In the united States, meanwhile, there is at least a

faint glimmer of hope in recent judicial rulings checking
Joe Biden's rogue 'unitary executive'. In November 2021,
the Fifth Circuit Court of Appeals cited "grave statutory
and Constitutional issues" as it blocked a vaccine
mandate by the Occupational Safety and Health
Administration (OSHA), which "grossly exceeded
OSHA's statutory authority." A few weeks later, Louisiana
federal judge Terry A. Doughty cited this ruling in his
own preliminary injunction against Biden's national
vaccine mandate for health-care workers.

As legal texts go, Doughty's injunction is an unusually
spirited document, upholding "the liberty of individuals
to make intensely personal decisions, even when those
decisions frustrate government officials." It rebuked the
administration's "arbitrary and capricious" mandate and
presumption of executive "superpowers," and schooled
Biden in elementary constitutional principles (albeit with
errant use of the word, 'laws').

> "If the separation of powers meant anything to the
> Constitutional framers, it meant that the three
> necessary ingredients to deprive a person of liberty or
> property—the power to make rules, to enforce them,
> and to judge their violations—could never fall into the
> same hands. If the Executive branch is allowed to usurp
> the power of the Legislative branch to make laws, two
> of the three powers conferred by the Constitution
> would be in the same hands.
>
> "If human nature and history teach anything, it is
> that civil liberties face grave risks when governments

proclaim indefinite states of emergency. During a pandemic such as this one, it is even more important to safeguard the separation of powers set forth in our Constitution to avoid erosion of our liberties."

If such sanity prevailed, this book would not need to exist, but what about the next 'emergency', or the one after that, when the false powers will resume their agenda of destruction and enslavement? We cannot afford to be complacent. We must keep our constitutional weapons sharp, our skills in wielding them finely honed, our verbal armour at hand.

PART III

OUR COMMON-LAW FOUNDATION

O good, my lord, no Latin....
The willing'st sin I ever yet committed
May be absolved in English.

— SHAKESPEARE, *KING HENRY VIII*

As we have seen, legislation passed by parliaments, along with decrees dictated by executive governments, can be violently at odds with constitutional and Rights protections. But legislation is overruled even more emphatically by Common Law, or 'Law of the Land', to which all are bound, whether man, woman, parliament, police, priest, or king.

In her no-nonsense book about Common Law, *Freedom Is More Than Just a Seven-Letter Word*, Veronica: of the Chapman family points out this Law of the Land "is the

only Law of the Land. And the only Law that needs to be obeyed on dry land."

As with constitutions, the beauty of Common Law rests in its common-sense simplicity, requiring us not to cause harm or loss to another and to conduct ourselves without mischief in promises and agreements. In short, **a crime is established when there is an injured party**.

"If there is no victim," explains Common-Law champion Chris Edward in a TikTok video, "if there is no-one with an affidavit or a statement against you to say you have caused them a loss, harm, or injury, where you've defrauded them or stolen something from them, if there is no human victim, there is no crime. If there is no crime, there is no fine."

"IF THERE IS NO VICTIM, THERE IS NO CRIME."

This is the reigning status in Common-Law nations, of which there are more than 40, including the U.K., along with other countries that used to be part of the British Empire, such as the united States, Canada, Australia, New Zealand, India, and Pakistan. This principle becomes especially powerful when dealing with would-be enforcers such as police.

As Anna de Buisseret explains in her Parliament Square interview, "We are a Common-Law jurisdiction in this country, and lots of countries around the world claim their jurisdiction from the U.K. And the Common-Law general principle is, '**First, do no harm**.' And what that means is that you don't get to harm anybody's person, property, liberty, etc." This phrase, which in Latin is "Primum non nocere," is supported in Common Law by "Voluntas aegroti suprema lex," de Buisseret adds, meaning, **"Over his or her mind or body, the individual is sovereign."**

Our status under Common Law is akin to diplomatic immunity, or the standing of foreign embassies, according to Darren (of the family) Deojee in the *Strawman* documentary: "Jurisdiction is portable. It's not tied to land, it's tied to the party, so I can carry my jurisdiction with me, which is the whole principle of sovereignty in general."

COMMON LAW OVERRULES LEGISLATION

The powers-that-shouldn't-be can make as many laws, decrees, regulations, rules, mandates or whatever they want, if these are not in alignment with Natural law, they are simply VOID from Inception, therefore UNAPPLICABLE and INEXISTENT in reality. Their 'power' exists only in a fake system of belief.

— DOM TREMBLAY, PRESENTATION AT
FREEDOM UNDER NATURAL LAW
CONFERENCE, FEB. 12, 2022

Common Law, or that which is 'lawful', is distinct from and superior to, that which is 'legal', meaning Acts and statutes implemented by legislatures. Naturally, it also overrules dictates and regulations issued by prime ministers and presidents and all who enjoy their patronage. As U.S. Supreme-Court judge Robert Jackson wrote in 1952, "With all its defects, delays and inconveniences, men have discovered no technique for long preserving free government except that the Executive be under the law."

But public and police alike have been fooled into believing Common Law and legislation are one and the same, according to former police officer Sarah (of the family) Feeley in the *Strawman* documentary, "so that when police are policing the streets, we're enforcing policies, Acts and statutes which, when looked into, are not necessarily lawful."

Common Law sets us free from legislation as surely as "The law of the Spirit of life in Christ Jesus hath made me free from the law of sin and death" (*Romans* 8:2). At the heart of Common Law is reverence for individual sovereignty wherein you are the supreme independent authority over your own body and your own territory. A government or parliament may suggest a set of rules and obligations to us, but under Common Law, it is up to each of us whether we accept it on an individual basis as a mutually agreed contract.

LEGISLATION ONLY BINDS US IF WE CONSENT TO IT WITH OUR SIGNATURE!

This concept is beautifully expressed in *Strawman*, as I quoted earlier…

"Parliament has no say in Common Law and is bound by it. So they create Acts of Parliament, and in the U.S.,

Acts of Congress. **Because government is a creation of man, and a creation of man can never be above man, they need your consent before they have the force of law."**

Or, as Jacquie Phoenix of Practical Lawful Dissent International puts it, **"We the people created government; they are the fiction… A fiction can never gain authority over its creator."**

Similarly, a building cannot have authority over its builder nor, for that matter, can a parliament building or any other 'Rathaus' of Europe have authority over the people. "A Builder can make a house. A house cannot make a Builder," explains Veronica in her book. "The Builder is 'above' the house. A Human Being can make a Law. The Law cannot make a Human Being. The Human Being is 'above' the Law."

But, she writes, "a very long time ago, the Countries, the Nations, were reorganized into CORPORATIONS, for the convenience of the Global Elite." Parliament, too, is a corporation, and its statutes are merely the 'legislated rules', or company policy, of the parent corporation. **As we never signed up to join this corporation, its legislated rules don't apply to us!**

This is where we part company with the state's attempt to enroll us as a corporate employee when it issued us with a Birth Certificate. This conjured a fictional 'citizen', also a corporate entity, and regarded us as human livestock in a tax farm. The Birth Certificate inducted us into a control system that regards Rights as privileges and claims ownership of our property through registration, deeming us mere users or 'keepers' of that property.

According to Common-Law advocate @joegcards in a TikTok broadcast, the Birth Certificate is not just a ploy to steal our Common-Law Birthright by enrolling us and enslaving us in a fraudulent system of 'Admiralty Law', but a traded stock. "You've been sold on the stock exchange," he asserts. "I can tell you what price you're trading at. When you find that out and know this, that money is actually yours."

Under Admiralty 'Law'—also known as Maritime 'Law', Fleet 'Law', Commerce 'Law', or 'Law' Merchant— we are deemed dead, 'lost at sea', meaning "they can plunder and pillage your ship, and take whatever gold you earn," says @joegcards. 'Earn' is a homonym of 'urn', he continues, a means to scatter our ashes, and 'earning' happens during the working week. By the weekend, we are 'weakened' and depleted.

And the telling homonyms don't stop there. We enter this world through a birth canal, but the Commerce system regards us as a ship given a 'berth'. Also, as riverbanks direct a river's current, institutional 'banks' direct the flow of currency.

The Admiralty system, you will observe, addresses correspondence to us with our name in ALL CAPS, as it would be engraved on a tombstone. This is deliberate. "Bills are addressed to a legal fiction, not a living man," says @joegcards. "I don't live on the sea, I live on the land. Maritime Law on land is treason, just like Acts and statutes." He concludes, "There are a lot of secrets in the British empire. We need to bring it down."

Another reason the state's Birth Certificate is fraudulent, and therefore void, is because it was done without the Full Disclosure that a Contract requires. Therefore, according to Veronica, "Bingo! You are free, because you say you are free!" We are delivered from the fictional legal entity of a citizen, and citizen 'ship', and from being a permanent debtor in a system of debts, fines, and taxes.

Veronica continues,

"After all, what is the Law, anyway? How does it come about? 'Consensus facit legem.' **Consent makes the Law.** The consent of the overwhelming majority, whose one primary desire is to live their lives in peace. In peaceful coexistence with everyone else. Free to do whatever it is they choose to do, provided they do not adversely affect anyone else. Free to travel at will. Free to express opinions. Free to exchange. And so on. Freedom from imposed fictions & illusions. Freedom from tyranny. Freedom from the domination of the many by the few.

"And those Common Sense desires were codified in Common Law, as a protection of it. And this was done many centuries ago. It formed the basis of the Magna Carta, the US Constitution, and so on. It actually forms the basis of every Constitution ever written. (Any Constitution worth its salt, that is.)...

"If you don't wear the Legal Fiction Person mask
then you are not a Member of THE UNITED
KINGDOM CORPORATION, and its rules don't apply
to you. Its Company Policy has no force of law upon
you. You can just walk away."

The same goes for other nation-corporations,
including the 'United States', which "means a Federal
corporation," as asserted in *United States Code* Title 28
Section 3002. Realizing this empowers our refusals. As de
Buisseret advises,

"It's as simple as saying 'no'. We are governed by
consent. So **if you don't consent to these measures,
they cannot force you to.** They might claim that they
can, but a lot of the cases that have gone to court have
been dropped because they're illegal. It's all just a
threat, a coercion, a way to make you comply."

For example, do you consent to being stopped and
searched without reasonable grounds, as the new U.K.
policing Bill presumes? No, neither do I. They may call it
'legal', but under Common Law, it is unlawful if
conducted without Consent and makes a criminal of any
police officer attempting to enforce it.

As Jacquie Phoenix explains, Acts and statutes can
only *add* protection to the people, not remove it. The
British monarch is supposed to deny Royal Assent to any
legislation that causes harm, loss, or fraud to the people
or that disrupts our peace. And even when Assent is

given, under Article 61 of *Magna Carta*, the legislation should still go before a jury of the people for approval.

Does *Magna Carta* still apply today? Absolutely! As Phoenix points out, "*Magna Carta* is a forever-binding document. That's clearly stated in Articles 1, 61, and 63." Article 1 states...

"TO ALL FREE MEN OF OUR KINGDOM we have also granted, for us and our heirs **for ever**, all the liberties written out below, and desire to be observed in good faith by our heirs **in perpetuity**."

I will honour the call of my ancestors, how about you? In Article 61, *Magna Carta* again states its provisions "shall be enjoyed in their entirety, **with lasting strength, for ever**." It closes with Article 63,

"that men in our kingdom shall have and keep all these liberties, rights, and concessions, well and peaceably **in their fullness and entirety** for them and their heirs, of us and our heirs, in all things and all places **for ever**. Both we and the barons have sworn that all this shall be observed in good faith and without deceit."

Thus, *Magna Carta* was thoroughly future-proofed to be not only permanent but intact, so that no future administration could pick and choose what it would honour and what it would not.

Bear in mind too, that this is the very same *Magna Carta* that then Queen Elizabeth II celebrated and described as "enduring" during eighth-centenary celebrations at Runnymede on June 15, 2015. Also present for the occasion was then prime minister David Cameron who asserted, "It is our duty to safeguard the legacy, the idea, the momentous achievement of those barons."

Well, neither he nor his successors nor predecessors have done so. And nor has the queen. Britain's **Coronation Oath** asks, "Will you to the utmost of your power maintain the Laws of God and the true profession of the Gospel?" This is a binding contract between the Crown and the people of the nation. But the queen gave automatic Assent to Acts of Parliament that are crimes under Common Law, without even reading them, and the people's juries have been ignored for centuries.

As a result, in Phoenix's words,

> "The criminals are just doing whatever they want, and the current regulations and things that we see today, they're all crimes against us, they're Common-Law crimes. They're causing us harm, they're causing us loss, they're breaching our peace. The fact that they've got us all listed as 'dead, lost at sea' is fraud against the people. So the government is currently committing all four Common-Law crimes against the people every single day before we've even had our morning cup of coffee."

So how do the most recent government actions over COVID appear in this context? "This is the largest corporate takeover of Humanity," Phoenix says, "which is all high treason."

And how do the pharmaceutical companies play into this treason? Article 61 also states:

> "We will not seek to procure from anyone, either by our own efforts or those of a third party, anything by which any part of these concessions or liberties might be revoked or diminished. Should such a thing be procured, it shall be null and void, and we will at no time make use of it, either ourselves or through a third party."

Well, Pfizer, AstraZeneca, and Moderna are third parties, aren't they? And hasn't a thing been procured from them that diminishes liberties? When will those things be rightly ruled "null and void"?

Caught courts

What about our so-called 'Judiciary' today? *Magna Carta* recognizes everyone's Right to Trial-by-Jury under Common Law, but courts without juries are 'de facto', according to Veronica, they are private companies, and we are "under no obligation whatsoever to accept any services any Company may have on offer." De-facto courts also expect us to stand in the 'dock' which, according to @joegcards, is an echo of Admiralty code by regarding us as a ship brought into dry dock on land.

Judges in these courts base their rulings on statutes

alone, and these statutes, as we have seen, have no authority over sovereign men and women. As Veronica observes, "it is impossible to adjudicate between Fictions (Persons/Corporations) and Reality (Humans). It is only possible to adjudicate between Fictions OR between Humans."

De-facto courts will sometimes stage a 'jury trial' but, as British Common-Law advocate, JP, points out in a newsletter, this is counterfeit. True trial-by-jury "reflects the truly ancient system of peer review of the evidence presented to support a claim; presumes innocence in the absence of a unanimous verdict; and IS the judge of both guilt and the justice of the Law cited in the claim."

But a 'jury trial', on the other hand,

"is a deliberate deceit, intended to sound like the above but framed entirely within the legal (not lawful) system of statute. The jury is not chosen from the defendant's peers; unanimity is never required; the 'judge' in the 'court' directs the jury; the jury will (generally) not consider the justice of the statute cited in the claim.

"Our constitution (yes, we have one) requires the former. Our legal system offers the latter. **The legal system tends to despotism**—judge, jury and executioner in one (legal) person—just as was overcome 808 years ago in the Great Charter."

Though I am a relative newcomer to Common-Law principles and what they mean for us, I have come to understand that, far from cowering before despotic politicians and wondering what new restriction or regulation they're going to hit us with next, we should be prosecuting them instead and, with the help of constables and military true to their oaths, seizing back our Birthright and our courts!

COMMON-LAW POLICING

The distinction between Common Law and 'lawful', versus legislation and 'legal', is especially important when it comes to police officers. Consider the **Oath for the Office of Constable** in Britain (included in Schedule 4 of the *Police Act* (1996), which applies to every police officer in England and Wales, irrespective of rank, as well as to British Transport and Ministry of Defence police...

"I do solemnly and sincerely declare and affirm that I will well and truly serve the Queen in the office of constable, with fairness, integrity, diligence and impartiality, **upholding fundamental human rights** and according equal respect to all people; and that I will, to the best of my power, cause the peace to be kept and preserved and prevent all offences against people and property; and that while I continue to hold the said office I will to the best of my skill and knowledge discharge all the duties thereof faithfully according to law."

And what does that final word, 'law', mean here? Not government legislation but Rights. As spelled out in the U.K. College of Policing *Code of Ethics*, "**You must uphold the law regarding human rights.**" Each officer also pledges under the Code to "give and carry out lawful orders only."

These statements are also rooted in *Magna Carta*: "We will appoint as justices, constables, sheriffs, or bailiffs only such as know the law of the realm and mean to observe it well" (Article 45). As is evident from countless videos online, people wearing police costumes these days spectacularly fail the *Magna-Carta* test. They neither know the Law nor observe it well. I, as the author of this book, and you as its reader, already know the Law far better than they. We are the true inheritors of Law and, if need be, its enforcers.

Remember, too, that police are a creation of Man, and that Man always has authority over his creation. In any interaction with police, therefore, *I* am the law, I have authority over them, and I am the one issuing *them* with 'lawful orders'. If I see cops behaving unlawfully or desecrating their oath, then, so help me God, I will arrest *them*!

Other jurisdictions using the phrase 'human rights' in police oaths are Scotland, Northern Ireland, and the Irish Garda. Northern Ireland's also includes "upholding the Constitution" and forbids membership of any secret society, while the Irish Garda's requires "equal respect to all individuals and their traditions and beliefs."

Canadian police swear in their **Oath**, "I will uphold the Constitution of Canada... and discharge my other duties as Police Constable, faithfully, impartially and according to law." The **Royal Canadian Mounted Police Act (RCMP Act)** also requires members "to respect the rights of all persons" and "to act at all times in a courteous, respectful and honourable manner" (Section 37). These declarations alone rebuke the brutal crackdown Canadian truckers endured in February 2022 at the hands and hooves of Ottawa police.

The Canadian police **Code of Conduct** also declares officers shall not "infringe or deny a person's rights or freedoms under the **Canadian Charter**," make any unlawful detention or arrest, "treat any person in a manner that is abusive or unprofessional," or "conduct themselves in a manner that undermines, or is likely to undermine, public trust in policing."[1] Well, the scars and bruises on the faces and bodies of peaceful dissenters in Ottawa tell a different story!

The oaths of Australian and New Zealand officers are disappointingly weak by comparison with the others cited. Though, in both cases, they must pledge to keep the peace and act "according to law," so help them God, neither mentions 'rights' or 'constitution'.

When Sir Robert Peel founded the British police force in 1829, officers were issued with nine Principles of Policing that detailed the meaning of 'Policing by Consent' and the idea that police are to regard themselves, and be regarded, as **citizens in uniform**. The Principles state "**that the police are the public and that the public are the police**, the police being only members of the public who are paid to give full-time attention to duties which are incumbent on every citizen in the interests of community welfare and existence."

The Principles also require officers "to use only the minimum degree of physical force which is necessary," "to refrain from even seeming to usurp the powers of the judiciary," and to make "ready offering of individual sacrifice in protecting and preserving life." There is no mention that police forces were ever intended as revenue-collection agencies which, as corporations, they have now become.

According to the Wiltshire Police Federation website, the Oath is sworn "to ensure the separation of power and **the political independence of the Office of Constable**." Officers "**are not agents of the police force, police authority or government. Each police officer has personal liability for their actions or inactions.**"

Let me repeat this, for it is not commonly understood, least of all by constables themselves...

POLICE OFFICERS ARE NOT, NOR EVER WERE, AGENTS OF GOVERNMENT

Let every officer, at every level, take this to heart when political figures summon them to enforce legislation or rulings that are either unconstitutional, or unlawful under Common Law. As the Nuremberg trials of 1945-1949 remind us, "I was just following orders" will never wash when Justice returns to the land.

This lesson is embraced by former Arizona sheriff, Richard Mack. "We have too many Nuremberg officers still in America and Canada, all across the world, that think we're just supposed to follow orders," he told Freedom Travel Alliance in a December 2021 interview. "We have no responsibility to obey unjust laws. Just the opposite... We will not enforce unjust laws. We will not be part of injustice. We will defend people's rights."

His mission, along with the Constitutional Sheriffs and Peace Officers Association (CSPOA), is to train 'peace officers' across the world to uphold Rights and their oaths of office, irrespective of legislation, and to protect the People against criminality by police, politicians, or judges.

The term 'peace officer' is also used in Canada's **RCMP Act** (1985) where "Every officer is a peace officer in every part of Canada." But the role may have its best chance in the united States because the post of Sheriff is filled by local election and not by political appointment.

Therefore, far from enforcing politicians' and bureaucrats' decrees without regard for constitutional protections, the job of police officers is to do the exact opposite: to protect us from those decrees.

"Acting as Peace Officers is what they are paid to do. I have no problem with that, and welcome it," writes Veronica. "Acting as Company Police Enforcement Officers (Policemen), enforcing the Law-of-Waters on dry land, and not realising it, and making absolutely no attempt to realise it, is where they have no authority, no jurisdiction, and are behaving in a grossly negligent manner. That's where the problem arises for me."

Also, as Anna de Buisseret points out in her Parliament-Square interview, officers have a Common-Law duty "to act to prevent harm. Omitting to act is as guilty as acting to cause harm."

Look up the oath sworn by police officers where you live. Look for language that mentions Common Law, Rights, constitutions, impartiality, without fear or favour, etc. Treasure these words, assert them, and share them, especially with those who have forgotten what they have sworn. To that end, you will find a letter in Appendix V for distribution to police officers at every level of command, which you can adapt for your particular location.

PART IV

OUR MEDICAL FOUNDATION

For being a shot in the arm, people sure are bending over and taking it in the ass.

— SHAWSHA NEWCOMB,
YOUTUBE COMMENT

We've all heard of the **Hippocratic Oath**, summarized as, "Do no harm." And that alone should demolish all the coercive medical measures and discrimination now being enacted by governments. The Oath also says, as set out in *Encyclopaedia Britannica,*

> "I will follow that system of regimen which, according to my ability and judgment, I consider for the benefit of my patients, and abstain from whatever is deleterious and mischievous. **I will**

give no deadly medicine to any one if asked, nor suggest any such counsel."

Are we clear? Also, as Dr Suneel Dhand points out in his popular online videos, a key element of medical ethics is individualised treatment, never 'one-size-fits-all'. But, as he laments, we have entered an age of medical absolutism in which assertion of individual sovereignty is considered heresy.

Therefore, as great swathes of the medical establishment appear to have forgotten their core values —following an oath hypocritical rather than Hippocratic —we will now revisit, revive, and reassert the medical Rights that have stood us in good stead in the millennia since Hippocrates.

MEDICAL EXPERIMENTATION

Front and centre, of course, is the *Nuremberg Code* (1947) pertaining to "medical experiments on human beings" and written to ensure these "conform to the ethics of the medical profession generally."

In the words of renowned cardiologist and epidemiologist, Dr. Peter McCullough, in a jaw-dropping interview with the DarkHorse podcast of Dec. 7, 2021, "Nuremberg Code says, under no conditions should anyone receive any pressure, coercion, or threat of reprisal for having something injected into their body as we apply it to vaccines in the setting of research—and that's what actually happened in Nazi Germany with the Nazi research program." Para. 1 of the *Code* begins,

> "**The voluntary consent of the human subject is absolutely essential**. This means that the person involved should have legal capacity to give consent;

should be so situated as to be able to exercise free power of choice, **without the intervention of any element of force, fraud, deceit, duress, overreaching, or other ulterior form of constraint or coercion**; and should have sufficient knowledge and comprehension of the elements of the subject matter involved as to enable him to make an understanding and enlightened decision."

No coercion? Then why was injection initially made a condition of employment for NHS staff—though, in the end, the government was forced to back down—and why were doctors like Kate Goodman, as she reports in a January 2022 interview, put under "extreme pressure from hospital management,... bullied and harassed" to get a COVID shot?

Listen to the irony in NHS Trust director Andy Beeby's response to her plight: "We are supporting our staff, giving people every opportunity to discuss concerns, and supporting them to make informed decisions."

That clueless bureaucrats can destroy the lives of others with such hollow and dishonest pleasantries, is one of the most frightening aspects of our society now.

The *Code*'s ten paragraphs also stipulate a medical experiment must be "based on the results of animal experimentation" and "a knowledge of the natural history of the disease." It should be "conducted only by scientifically qualified persons," "**protect the experimental subject against even remote possibilities of injury, disability or death**," and be terminated as soon as any of these outcomes appears likely.

Even a perfunctory analysis will confirm that none of these requirements has been fulfilled for the products rushed to market by Pfizer, Moderna, AstraZeneca, and Johnson & Johnson in response to COVID. In the words of McCullough, "Our vaccine program would have been shut down in January [2021] for excess mortality... People aren't willing to sacrifice their lives for this, and that's what they're being asked for."

It amounts to "a giant abdication of medical ethics, of pharmacovigilance, and regulatory principles. And it's extraordinarily dangerous. I think historians will write about this for years to come. How did America go off the rails?"

You can find violations of **Nuremberg** in official government papers, such as the British government's aforementioned excuse for a 'Consultation Document' about the rollout of injections, originally published Aug. 28, 2020. Apart from issuing pre-emptive legal immunity for pharmaceutical companies and all in the supply chain, it paved the way for "unlicensed products," "vaccine promotion," and "expansion of the workforce eligible to administer vaccinations," such as NHS-contracted providers and the armed forces.

Suspiciously, the original text of this Consultation Document has been altered since its first appearance, a chilling reminder of Orwell's 'Memory Hole' of *1984*, where inconvenient history is cut from news archives and replaced with a narrative more aligned with the Party's fictions. Even so, the most recent iteration begins with its original falsehoods: that COVID "is the biggest threat this country has faced in peacetime history," and that vaccines "will be the best way to deal with the pandemic."

Nuremberg is also cited by British doctor Lucie Wilk in her searing Nov. 15, 2021 article, *Why have we doctors been silent?*, which denounces the British medical establishment's complicity in vaccine imperialism, especially when these products were still in experimental stages. "Despite our training to look at scientific literature and data with a critical eye," she writes, "the silence from the medical community in the UK has been deafening. Yet we are the ones who should be shouting all of this from the rooftops. This is a duty of care and an oath we have forgotten."

Our protective medical codes do not stop with *Nuremberg*. In 1964, the World Medical Association issued the *Declaration of Helsinki – Ethical Principles for Medical Research Involving Human Subjects*. It is worth reading all 37 of its paragraphs, but I pick out a couple for their particular relevance today. Para. 9 states, "It is the duty of physicians who are involved in medical research to protect the life, health, dignity, integrity, **right to self-determination, privacy, and confidentiality of personal information of research subjects.**" And Para. 15 adds, "Appropriate compensation and treatment for subjects who are harmed as a result of participating in research must be ensured."

It is not hard to find tragic examples where *Nuremberg* and *Helsinki* have been desecrated. At a U.S. Senate hearing on vaccine injuries conducted by Senator Ron Johnson on Nov. 2, 2021, Stephanie de Garay described how her daughter Maddie, aged 12 at the time, was paralyzed from the waist down after participating in Pfizer's vaccine trials for adolescents at Cincinnati Children's Hospital.

About 18 hours after receiving her second Pfizer dose on Jan. 20, 2021, Maddie developed severe nerve pain, a feeling like electric shocks going down her neck and spine, excruciating abdominal pain, and severe chest pain that felt like her heart was being pulled out. Her vaccine arm swelled up and became numb. Her fingers and toes turned white, and were ice cold to the touch. The pain in her toes was so extreme that she had to walk on her heels.

Over the following months, Maddie's condition worsened, including food regurgitation and vomiting, until she was unable to swallow any food or liquids, and had to resort to a feeding tube. The pain throughout her body persisted, especially in her abdomen, which became distended. She experienced fainting spells which developed into seizures, sometimes ten a day.

Prior to injection, Maddie had never menstruated, but on Feb. 5, 2021, she started to discharge brown fluid, which came out in chunks over the following month. Painful cysts developed on her vagina and then her head. Erratic blood pressure and heart rate were also among the symptoms, along with tinnitus, vision problems, headaches, dizziness, and memory loss. Finally, she lost feeling from the waist down, which led to paralysis and incontinence.

Nuremberg states, "During the course of the experiment the scientist in charge must be prepared to terminate the experiment at any stage, if he has probable cause to believe, in the exercise of the good faith, superior skill and careful judgment required of him, that a continuation of the experiment is likely to result in injury, disability, or death to the experimental subject" (Para. 10).

But Dr. Robert Frenck, who headed Maddie's trial at Cincinnati Children's Hospital, did not terminate the experiment. In his lead-authored article about the trial, published in *The New England Journal of Medicine* (*NEJM*) in May 2021, we learn that it ran until Mar. 13, 2021 (p.2), almost two months after Maddie got her second Pfizer shot.

Worse yet, Frenck asserted in the article that Pfizer's vaccine "had a favorable safety and side-effect profile... there were no vaccine-related serious adverse events and few overall severe adverse events" (p.1). Then he added yet more insult to Maddie's injuries when, in a May 17, 2021 phone call with her parents, he said Pfizer would not cover the staggering medical bills the family had run up at Cincinnati Children's in coping with the results of Maddie's second dose. "The doctors that have seen her so far have not found something where they thought it was research related," he said, meaning his team deemed Maddie's injuries unattributable to the clinical trial.

Maddie's debilitation was recorded in trial data as "abdominal pain," though even this was a criminal understatement as she would scream in agony from that one symptom alone. Stephanie filed a report on Maddie's behalf with the Vaccine Adverse Event Reporting System (VAERS), a database jointly managed by the FDA and the CDC, but "Neither Pfizer, the FDA, or the CDC has ever talked to us or attempted to," she told Senator Johnson's hearing. "We have never heard anything from them."

Preschool teacher Brianne ('Bri') Dressen also spoke at the hearing, along with several more men and women whose tears alone testified to Big Pharma's wanton devastation of life and even the will to live. Bri suffered devastating neurological damage after receiving her first dose in AstraZeneca's clinical trial in 2020, forcing her early withdrawal before a second dose could be given. "The heads of the NIH, FDA, and CDC have known first-hand about my case and thousands of others," she reported. "We have literally asked and we have begged repeatedly for them to acknowledge these reactions. They declined." Nor were any regulators present at the hearing. Like the vaccine manufacturers and mainstream news outlets, they ignored invitations to attend.

AstraZeneca was operating from the same playbook in the U.K., where its clinical trial was suspended in September 2020 after it produced "severe neurological symptoms consistent with transverse myelitis, or inflammation of the spinal cord," a development revealed not by press release but in a CEO call with investors. The same condition later paralyzed Doug Cameron, another witness at the hearing, who got the Johnson & Johnson shot in April 2021.

So how did the U.K. regulator respond when the AstraZeneca trial went awry? Britain's Medicines for Human Use (Clinical Trials) Regulations of 2004 are supposed to ensure 'good clinical practice', and the licensing authority is empowered to shut down any trial that fails to, but this one was resumed again within days of the suspension. I can only imagine how the parties involved justified to themselves this circumvention of medical protocol and, let's face it, common sense!

MEDICAL TREATMENT

And now we reach the crux of this book, the overthrow of vaccine mandates which, as family physician Dr Charles Hoffe points out, "are slavery" because the government "are claiming ownership over your body." He was forced out of his job in British Columbia, Canada after defending medical sovereignty for himself and his patients.

As we have seen, *Nuremberg* and *Helsinki* apply to experimental medicine. Does that mean post-experimental medical treatments would be any less subject to patient consent? Hell, no!

At a foundational level, the *UDHA* recognizes our **"security of person"** (Article 3), while "the right of **self-determination**" is enshrined in the *ICESCR* (Article 1).

The constitutions of individual nations affirm these Rights. In the united States of America, the **Fourth Amendment** protects "The right of the people to be secure in their persons...." Similarly, the *Canadian Bill of*

Rights (1960) lists among fundamental freedoms the Right of the individual to "security of the person" (Part I, Section 1(a)).

But perhaps our strongest sanctuary of all is the *Universal Declaration on Bioethics and Human Rights* (2005) (***UDBHR***) which states, "**any preventive, diagnostic and therapeutic medical intervention is only to be carried out with the prior, free and informed consent of the person concerned,** based on adequate information" (Article 6).

If you print out only one Rights document of the many listed in this book, I recommend this one. The ***UDBHR*** may be the most powerful key in these times, for it means no-one can be coerced or compelled to wear a mask or receive an injection ("preventive") or to take a medical test ("diagnostic") without their consent. In short,...

UNDER INTERNATIONAL LAW, NO-ONE MAY DEMAND WE WEAR A MASK, GET A TEST, OR BE INJECTED WITHOUT CONSENT.

Australia, where government agents raided the offices of doctors who issued vaccine exemptions, merits particular attention. The **Australian Constitution** forbids government provision of medical and dental services with "any form of **civil conscription**" (Section 51.23A).

Europeans have targeted protection with *Resolution 2361*, passed by the Parliamentary Assembly of the

Council of Europe on Jan. 27, 2021, which resolves that member states and the European Union "Ensure that citizens are informed that the vaccination is **NOT mandatory** and that no one is politically, socially, or otherwise pressured to get themselves vaccinated if they do not wish to do so" (Paragraph 7.3.1).

The following paragraph resolves that these nations "Ensure that no one is discriminated against for not having been vaccinated due to possible health risks **or not wanting to be vaccinated**" (Paragraph 7.3.2).

But in these lawless times, European leaders are paying no heed. Among the most glaring violations is Austria where, in November 2021, Chancellor Alexander Schallenberg announced vaccination would be a legal requirement from Feb. 1, 2022.

Then, in December 2021, Greek prime minister Kyriakos Mitsotakis announced, "vaccination is henceforth compulsory" for Greeks over the age of 60, and any who refused would pay monthly fines. This from the birthplace of democracy? From the land that Spartans defended at Thermopylae, and Athenians shielded with their navy at Salamis?

The U.K., which is one of 47 member states in the Council of Europe (with or without 'Brexit'), has additional medical safeguards of its own, including the one good thing to be added in the latest revisions to the aforementioned *Public Health (Control of Disease) Act*. Section 45E states (as of Nov. 7, 2021), "Regulations under section 45B or 45C **may not include provision requiring a person to undergo medical treatment.**

'Medical treatment' includes vaccination and other prophylactic treatment."

What are sections 45B and 45C? These are the tyrannical edicts already examined and despised above, where the 'appropriate Minister' may play the role of unaccountable king. Nevertheless, when it comes to vaccines, as British charity Liberty point out, the Act "specifically prevents ministers from creating new rules which would make vaccines mandatory."

Even so, the new sections of the Act presume a minister may impose medical examination and "disinfection" of persons. This contradicts the NHS' own *Constitution* which states, "You have the right to accept or refuse treatment that is offered to you, and not to be given any physical examination or treatment unless you have given valid consent." The NHS website also states,

> "Consent to treatment means a person must give permission before they receive **any type of medical treatment, test, or examination.** This must be done on the basis of an explanation by a clinician. Consent from a patient is needed regardless of the procedure, whether it's a physical examination, organ donation or something else. **The principle of consent is an important part of medical ethics and international human rights law.**"

And that consent, the NHS specifies, must be "voluntary," a factor conspicuously absent from the U.K. rollout of COVID injections, which many people took under duress so they could continue to feed themselves or their families, to travel, or see relatives. As de Buisseret notes, "They didn't give their consent freely. There were coerced, they were threatened, they were intimidated, they were sanctioned, they were guilt-tripped."

Uninformed consent

As we have seen, the **UDBHR** requires not just consent for any medical intervention but *informed* consent. Any potential recipient of any treatment, test, or examination must be informed of risks and alternative treatments. As the U.K. Medical Freedom Alliance points out, "you should be presented with arguments for and against each of the options."

The bar is so high for this that even a patient's signature is insufficient to affirm they were informed, as the U.K.-based Medical Protection Society explains on its website: "If there is any dispute over whether valid consent was obtained, the key issue will not be whether the patient signed a form or not, but whether they were given all the information they needed to make a considered decision."

But injectees in the U.K. and elsewhere never had the benefit of a second opinion. Deeming us too stupid to weigh our own choices, the medical establishment strove to shield us from any grain of doubt that their new and experimental serums were the only viable option. Injectors across the nation neglected to tell recipients they would be participating in a medical experiment and clinical trial, that animals had died from prior experiments with similar products, or that trial subjects had experienced anaphylactic shock, inflammation of the spinal cord, paralysis, and Bell's palsy, which causes half of a person's face to droop. All of these symptoms had appeared before the public rollout had begun!

Nor were patients informed of alternative treatments. On the contrary, alternatives were aggressively censored and suppressed. As Robert F. Kennedy Jr., author of *The Real Anthony Fauci*, points out in a December 2021 interview with political comedian Jimmy Dore, emergency-use authorization of vaccines is prohibited under U.S. legislation "if there is an existing medication that has been approved for *any* purpose that shows it's effective against the target illness." Therefore, **any official acknowledgement of alternative COVID treatments would have caused the entire vaccine program to collapse.**

All this has been orchestrated in a climate of manufactured fear that shuts down rational analysis and thought. As de Buisseret comments, "Not a single person in the U.K. is able to give their informed consent due to the military-grade psychological warfare that's being conducted on them, let alone children. Now, what that means is that no consent that's been obtained is lawful or legal."

This makes U.K. vaccinators criminally liable under Sections 20 and 47 of the *Offences Against the Person Act* (1861), carrying prison sentences up to seven years and two years, respectively. "The moment you pierce someone's skin," says de Buisseret, "that's a wound. You've just conducted a live human experiment on someone by wounding them, and anything that happens to them will therefore be your personal civil and criminal liability."

The only conclusion to be drawn amid the bewildering impositions of this age is that entire echelons of our government, civil service, and legislature, along with the medical, corporate, and security establishments, are criminally liable en masse for a barrage of physical and psychological assaults on their own populations.

They would do better to echo what South African president Cyril Ramaphosa said on Feb. 1, 2021 as his nation received its first doses:

> "Nobody will be forced to take this vaccine. I want to repeat. Nobody will be forced to take this vaccine. Nobody will be forbidden from travelling to wherever they want to travel to, including from enrolling at school or from taking part in any public activity if they have not been vaccinated. Nobody will be given this vaccine against their will."

Or Japan's Ministry of Health, which says on its website, "No vaccination will be given without consent. Please do not force anyone in your workplace or those around you to be vaccinated, and do not discriminate against those who have not been vaccinated."

I find it baffling how any political actor would assert

bodily autonomy and the 'Right to Choose' when it comes to abortion, but deny it when it comes to injections. And why they would mandate the involuntary insertion of pricks when, in another context, this is rape, or *persuade* insertion of pricks through fear and manipulation when, in another context, this is grooming? Even as I write this, I can hear the anger and denouncements my questions will provoke, but if they have this effect on you, why not try to answer them honestly?

Children

> *You shall not give any of your children to devote them by fire to Molech, and so profane the name of your God.*
>
> — *LEVITICUS* 18:21

Prohibitions against medical enforcement are especially compelling, and the Crimes Against Humanity especially grievous, when it comes to the child who, as recognized in the U.N. *Convention on the Rights of the Child* (1989) (*UNCRC*), "needs special safeguards and care, including appropriate legal protection, before as well as after birth." And in Britain, the *Serious Crime Act* (2015) specifies that the offence of child cruelty "covers **cruelty which causes psychological suffering or injury as well as physical harm.**"

But, far from protecting children, governments and

Big Pharma raced to pierce their vulnerable bodies with experimental serums. In May 2021, the FDA extended Emergency-Use Authorization (EUA) for Pfizer's injection down to 12-year-olds, then to five-year-olds in October 2021. In supporting the latter, Dr Eric Rubin, a member of the FDA's advisory committee, and editor-in-chief at the *New England Journal of Medicine*, infamously said, "We're never going to learn about how safe the vaccine is unless we start giving it. That's just the way it goes."

If real-world results were truly the benchmark for Rubin to evaluate vaccine safety, he could have found clear and overwhelming evidence of harm long ago, not just by extrapolating the death and destruction already doled out to older age groups, but by looking at the devastation already inflicted on the youngest recipients who had been prematurely injected before the authorizations reached their age group.

In May 2021, the FDA formally received Pfizer's Biological Product File, including its clinical-trial data, as the company applied for official licensure, or 'approval', of its serum, instead of mere 'authorization'. Pfizer achieved this status on Aug. 23, 2021.

Comprising hundreds of thousands of pages later wrested from the FDA through intense legal action and then released to the public, the file includes an explosive document titled *Cumulative Analysis of Post-Authorization Adverse Event Reports of PF-07302048 (BNT162B2) Received Through 28-Feb-21*.

This *Cumulative Analysis* document tallies adverse-event reports Pfizer received from 63 countries between December 2020, when regulators began issuing their authorizations, and the close of February 2021. No child was supposed to receive a Pfizer shot during that reporting period, but Pfizer knew of 34 children, aged between two months and nine years, who did. Twenty-nine of them were in the U.K.

Of the 34 children, 24 experienced at least one serious adverse event (p.13). One was "a 7-year-old female subject who received the vaccine and had stroke (unknown outcome); no follow-up is possible for clarification" (p.25). Yet Pfizer's paper concludes, "No new significant safety information was identified based on a review of these cases compared with the non-paediatric population" (p.13).

Should we be comforted by this language, telling us the outcomes for children were no worse than the outcomes for adults? Not when the document counted 1,223 post-injection deaths among all age groups (p.7). These numbers, shocking as they are, represent but a sample of the total because, as the document notes, "Reports are submitted voluntarily, and the magnitude of underreporting is unknown" (p.5).

Childhood harms and deaths were also showing up early in the vastly underreported VAERS. A targeted search of the database finds more than 100 cases of serious injury in under-15s by Apr. 30, 2021...

From the 8/11/2023 release of VAERS data:

Found 117 cases where Age is under-15 and Vaccine is COVID19 and Serious and Vaccination Date on/before '2021-04-30'

Government Disclaimer on use of this data

Table

Age	Count	Percent
< 6 Months	17	14.53%
6-11 Months	5	4.27%
1-2 Years	12	10.26%
3-5 Years	8	6.84%
6-17 Years	75	64.1%
TOTAL	117	100%

They include...

- A one-month-old girl diagnosed with Guillain-Barré syndrome, meaning her immune system was attacking her own nervous system and destroying the myelin sheath coating nerves. She lost sensation in her hands and feet and had breathing difficulties after a Pfizer shot (VAERS ID: 1067714).

- A two-month-old boy who went into cardiac arrest the same day he received a Pfizer dose. "No follow-up attempts possible. No further information expected" (VAERS ID: 1015467).

- A four-month-old boy diagnosed with myocarditis, where the heart muscle becomes inflamed and thereby weakened, 18 days after he was Pfizer-jabbed (VAERS ID: 1113390).

- A one-year-old boy who went into convulsions and seizure two days after a Moderna shot, and died (VAERS ID: 1261766).

- A two-year-old boy diagnosed with Bell's palsy one week after a first Pfizer dose (VAERS ID: 1234413).

- A two-year-old girl who died four days after a second Pfizer dose "during Pfizer's COVID-19 vaccine experiments on children" (VAERS ID: 1297169).

- A three-year-old girl who went into spasms about five hours after Pfizer (VAERS ID: 984229).

- A three-year-old child (gender unknown) who started having hallucinations three days after Moderna, with "uncontrolled thoughts of being stalked raped hearing voices." For some reason, the child was given a second dose of Moderna, after which the psychosis escalated (VAERS ID: 1294861).

- A six-year-old boy who went into anaphylactic shock five minutes after Pfizer. "The patient was hospitalized and condition was considered life-threatening" (VAERS ID: 999492).

- A six-year-old boy who developed vertigo and an "alarming" loss of balance after Moderna (VAERS ID: 1314766).

- A seven-year-old girl who went into a confused state with decreased mobility after she got a Pfizer shot. "The overall decline of the patient on an unspecified date since the first dose has been rapid and distressing to watch. The reporter has no doubt it was connected to the

vaccine. She has just got the second vaccine today. The reporter will be monitoring the patient's reaction very closely. The events were reported as serious, disability... The patient had not recovered from the events. No follow-up attempts are possible"
(VAERS ID: 1050594).

But the FDA didn't let any of these outcomes interfere with its reckless race to the cradle. By November 2021, Moderna was being trialed in six-month-old babies. Finally, the FDA extended EUAs for both Pfizer and Moderna shots down to six-month-olds on June 17, 2022.

At the following press conference, Dr. Peter Marks, director of the FDA's Center for Biologics Evaluation and Research (CBER), asserted that the 'vaccines' were "safe and effective for use in our nation's youngest children." Note that he said this more than a year after the FDA received Pfizer's devastating *Cumulative Analysis* report and more than a year after all the VAERS cases I listed above.

Reading from a teleprompter, he continued, "The FDA was acutely aware of the trust bestowed on it by the American people." Parents, caregivers, and health-care providers could "trust that both of these vaccines have been authorized with science and safety at the forefront of our minds."

Pfizer would have gone even younger if it could, as I discovered in another paper in the Biological Product File titled *License Action Recommendation Documents*. There, an entry for July 20, 2021 shows Pfizer was in talks with the FDA about "another study to enroll infants <6 months of age" (p.10).

20-JUL-2021 Y Telecon. Information Request - Clinical IR for a revised pediatric plan to include study C4591007 for subject 6 months to 11 years of age and proposal of another study to enroll infants <6 months of age. (NAIK, RAMACHANDRA)

What kind of informed consent is that?! It is child sacrifice. It is the idolatrous worship of Molech. It is an abomination in the eyes of God and Man. It is service to a cult, a cult blind to facts, reason, and truth, blind to Rights, and deaf to the Spirit's call in our hearts.

As Robert F. Kennedy, Jr. explained in another December 2021 interview, pharmaceutical companies *need* to inject children to prolong legal immunity.

"The Emergency-Use Authorization vaccines have liability protection under the PREP Act and under the CARES Act. So as long as you take an emergency use, you can't sue them. Once they get approved, now you can sue them unless they can get it recommended for children, because **all vaccines that are officially recommended for children get liability protection, even if an adult gets that vaccine.** That's why they're going after kids. They know this is going to kill and injure a huge number of children, but they need to do it for the liability protection."

Meanwhile, in September 2021, the U.K.'s then prime minister Boris Johnson, and then health secretary Sajid

Javid, overruled the government's own Joint Committee for Vaccination and Immunisation (JCVI) after it refused to recommend jabs for healthy 12- to 15-year-olds. This reversal violates the "Obligation on the Secretary of State to ensure implementation of JCVI recommendations," set out in Britain's *Health Protection (Vaccination) Regulations* (2009).

As the **ICCPR** declares, "The family is the natural and fundamental group unit of society and is entitled to protection by society and the State" (Article 23). But, in their rush to roll out red-carpet treatment for Big Pharma, governments are even setting aside parental consent, allowing children to get injected behind their parents' backs. GB News host, Neil Oliver, said of these developments in August 2021,

"I say this is worse than madness, that it is wickedly wrong. Over and above the safety or not, the efficacy or not, of experimental injections rolled out under the terms of Emergency Use Authorization and for which we have no long-term data, I am scared to the pit of my stomach by any government that seeks to come between parent and child…

"Governments, if they know what's good for them, stay the hell away from law-abiding parents and their kids. Down through history, one totalitarian regime after another, one ideology after another, has identified the family as the fundamental building block of society and thereby the most stubborn stumbling block on the road to establishing their brave new worlds. Those ideologies and regimes that seek total control over the lives of populations, always seek to undermine the family. 'Give me the child until he's seven,' as the saying goes, 'and I will show you the man.' As I say, I call that madness, wickedness, and I say that it scares me the most."

MEDICAL TESTING

I am writing this book primarily as a response to vaccine mandates, which do great violence to medical Rights. For me, as for millions of others who went along with masking requirements for a grudging while, vaccines are the last straw, the line that must not be crossed. But what of compulsory testing which, as we have seen, is included in revisions to the U.K. *Public Health Act*, whereby a minister may impose medical examination, detention, isolation, and quarantine?

Again, the **UDBHR** is our rock as it enforces prior, free, and informed consent for "diagnostic" interventions too. In short, there is to be **NO TESTING WITHOUT CONSENT**. The NHS' own definition of Consent says, "a person must give permission before they receive any type of medical treatment, **test, or examination.**" Therefore, as Lawyers for Liberty counsel, consent to diagnostic intervention "must be freely given without pressure or undue influence."

These findings also mean any employer who enforces COVID testing as a condition of employment or "strongly recommends" it, is behaving coercively and in violation of Consent.

MEDICAL CONFIDENTIALITY

There will be, in the next generation or so, a pharmacological method of making people love their servitude, and producing dictatorship without tears, so to speak, producing a kind of painless concentration camp for entire societies, so that people will in fact have their liberties taken away from them, but will rather enjoy it, because they will be distracted from any desire to rebel by propaganda or brainwashing, or brainwashing enhanced by pharmacological methods. And this seems to be the final revolution.

— ALDOUS HUXLEY

Close cousin to Informed Consent is Medical Confidentiality.

IF THIS ONE PRINCIPLE WERE RESPECTED, THEN ANY COERCION OR DISCRIMINATION

BASED ON MEDICAL STATUS WOULD BE IMPOSSIBLE.

The Right to Medical Confidentiality is rooted in the Right to Privacy. The **UDHR** states, "No one shall be subjected to arbitrary interference with his **privacy**, family, home or correspondence" (Article 12).

This is echoed in Article 8 of the *European Convention on Human Rights* (ECHR), where "Everyone has the right to respect for his private and family life, his home and his correspondence," and in national constitutions such as the *Canadian Charter* with "the right to be secure against unreasonable search or seizure" (Section 8). Similarly, in the united States of America, the **Fourth Amendment** of the *Bill of Rights* states,

> "The right of the people to be secure in their persons, houses, papers, and effects, against unreasonable searches and seizures, shall not be violated, and no Warrants shall issue, but upon probable cause, supported by Oath or affirmation, and particularly describing the place to be searched, and the persons or things to be seized."

This means your medical status, including of course your immunization status and any documentation pertaining to your medical status, is nobody else's business. It is not the government's business, it is not your employer's business, it is not a travel company's business, and it is not your neighbour's business. Nor is it Google's business as it harvests your Internet searches about medical conditions to sell your data to the highest bidder. If anyone demands to know your medical status, they have to go to court and get a Warrant. No statute or regulation can sidestep this.

So we have a ready instrument if facing unlawful demands in the united States to disclose vaccination status. Even if you are a visitor or immigrant, demand a Warrant, for the Fourth Amendment applies to "the people," and people come in various nationalities.

And what do the medical codes themselves have to say about confidentiality? A physician's pledge to keep our information confidential has been central to the practice of medicine from the beginning, including the *Hippocratic Oath* excerpted before, which states,

"Whatever I see or hear in the life of men which ought not to be spoken of abroad, whether in connection with my professional practice or not, **I will not divulge**, as reckoning that all such should be kept secret."

"I WILL NOT DIVULGE."

Helsinki also embodies "**privacy, and confidentiality of personal information of research subjects**" (Para. 9).

And again, the *UDBHR* also proves a tower of strength: "**The privacy of the persons concerned and the confidentiality of their personal information should be respected**" (Article 9). That means information collected by healthcare professionals is never to be divulged to politicians, bureaucrats, corporations, employers, travel companies, police, army, or anyone else.

In the U.K., the **NHS** *Code of Practice* (2003) states that, as established in case precedent and professional codes of conduct, "**A duty of confidence** arises when one person discloses information to another (e.g. patient to clinician)," and that practitioners must ensure the public "give their consent for the disclosure and use of their personal information."

This applies even to sharing information between healthcare professionals.

> "Sometimes, if patients choose to **prohibit information being disclosed to other health professionals** involved in providing care, it might mean that the care that can be provided is limited and, in extremely rare circumstances, that it is not possible to offer certain treatment options."

So, if physicians may not share confidential patient information even among themselves without the patient's consent, then certainly no-one in Government nor any enforcer has any business demanding it.

Again, all this demolishes the pretensions of the revised U.K. *Public Health Act*, which assumes a minister may require persons "to provide information or answer questions (including information of questions relating to their health)." No, he most certainly may not!

Therefore, let us all be sovereign in this. Nowadays, I

won't answer even casual enquiries about my medical status or medical history, but reply that I'm upholding medical confidentiality. For one thing, there is far too much riding on it, and people seem to have forgotten that personal medical information is sacred. I suggest you remind them!

MEDICAL DISCRIMINATION

All animals are equal, but some animals are more equal than others.

— GEORGE ORWELL, *ANIMAL FARM*

Given that our medical information is sacrosanct and confidential, medical discrimination on the basis of it should be impossible. I shouldn't even have to write this section. How can you discriminate against people on the basis of medical status when you don't even know what that status is?

But as we see, the tyrants are acquiring and sharing data that doesn't belong to them and using it to impose apartheid systems, scapegoating the unvaccinated, and fomenting hatred against sovereign people as spreaders of disease, a claim easily refuted when uncorrupted science is allowed to do its job. Some doctors and hospitals are even unlawfully withholding medical treatment for unrelated issues, based on a person's standing according to the COVID dictatorship.

And though all this demonization of the unvaccinated is itself demonic, illogical, and unscientific, it is grooming the gullible to go along with any atrocity against their brethren, whether by state or mob, in the name of staying 'safe'.

I often envisage the architects of this villainy as greedy, bloated frogs lording it over an evaporating puddle of tadpoles while sucking the water out, lest their kin should survive to enjoy the same benefits. Then persuading the tadpoles that their woes are the fault of another group of tadpoles, inciting them to blame and turn against each other, rather than attribute their suffering to the self-exalted amphibious overlords. I have written a short fable based on this idea, *The Parable of the Frogs*, which you can find at my Substack account, poetseye.substack.com.

But international Rights declarations are on the side of the tadpoles. As the **UDHA** declares, "Everyone is entitled to all the rights and freedoms set forth in this Declaration, without distinction of any kind, such as race, colour, sex, language, religion, political or other **opinion**, national or social origin, property, birth or **other status**" (Article 2). And "All are entitled to equal protection against any discrimination" (Article 7).

This "other status" language also appears in **ICESCR**

(Part II, Article 2, Para. 2) and in *UNCRC* (Article 2) applying to children, whether that status is the child's or its parents.

These protections are further bolstered by the *Rome Statute* of the International Criminal Court (1998), which includes **"persecution against any identifiable group"** in its list of 'Crimes against humanity' (Article 7).

Yet that is exactly what French president Emmanuel Macron did in January 2022 when he said he would reduce the minority of the unvaccinated "by pissing them off even more" and "by limiting, as much as possible, their access to activities in social life."

Similar happened in Israel, as pointed out by Professor Ehud Qimron, head of Microbiology and Immunology at Tel Aviv University. In a January 2022 open letter to the Israel Ministry of Health, he wrote,

> "You branded, without any scientific basis, people who chose not to get vaccinated as enemies of the public and as spreaders of disease. You promote, in an unprecedented way, a draconian policy of discrimination, denial of rights and selection of people, including children, for their medical choice. A selection that lacks any epidemiological justification."

Europeans, including British people, are also guarded by *ECHR*, which in Article 14 prohibits discrimination "on any ground, such as sex, race, colour, language, religion, political or **other opinion**, national or social origin, association with a national minority, property, birth or **other status.**"

Furthermore, the European Court of Human Rights, which ultimately adjudicates *ECHR*, confirms in its published *Guidance* on Article 14 that it applies to "discrimination based on disability, **medical conditions** or genetic features" (Para. 164).

The key distillation for our purposes is:

NONE MAY DISCRIMINATE AGAINST US BASED ON MEDICAL STATUS!

And that status, of course, includes whether or not we are vaccinated. The *Guidance* goes on to say...

"As regards discrimination against people with infectious diseases, the Court has considered that a distinction made on account of an individual's health status, including such conditions as HIV infection, should also be covered – either as a disability or a form thereof – by the term 'other status' in the text of Article 14 of the Convention" (Para. 171).

Among its case studies, the *Guidance* cites I.B. v. Greece, 2013, in which the Court determined a violation had occurred with "dismissal from work of an employee suffering from HIV infection" (Para. 208).

British people are also protected by this because the U.K. *Human Rights Act* (1998) (HRA) adopts *ECHR*, and 'Brexit' has not changed that. As the Oxford

Constitutional Law website explains, the Act "gives direct domestic effect to the UK's obligations under the European Convention on Human Rights (ECHR). **Any public executive action, including statutory instruments, that violate Convention rights is unlawful**... There was no decision to derogate from the ECHR, or any other international convention" (Paras. 9 and 10).

Even on a stand-alone basis, the *HRA* enshrines Rights and freedoms "without discrimination on any ground such as sex, race, colour, language, religion, political or other opinion, national or social origin, association with a national minority, property, birth or **other status** (Article 14).

Also, the U.K. *Equality Act* (2010) specifically protects us from discrimination by public bodies and service providers such as police. Its 'protected characteristics' include religion and belief.

British police must also comply with the *Public Sector Equality Duty* (2011) (PSED), requiring them in all decisions and policies to "eliminate discrimination, harassment, victimisation and any other conduct that is prohibited by or under the Equality Act 2010." But more than that, police officers must "**take a proactive approach to opposing discrimination**," as asserted in the U.K. College of Policing's aforementioned *Code of Ethics*.

Continental drift

So how well are European politicians doing when it comes to medical discrimination? Abysmally! By the time of writing, Austria had ordered a national lockdown that applied only to unvaccinated people; Germany required its citizens to show COVID passes in workplaces and on buses and trains, and Macron had told French citizens, "Vaccinate yourself so that you can lead a normal life... Being free in a nation like France entails being responsible and showing solidarity."

Sickening that he or any other political figure should regard vaccine compliance as a ticket to 'freedom', forgetting that freedom is inalienable, not something to be bestowed or withheld at government whim.

In the U.K., Boris Johnson was similarly mafioso when, on Nov. 16, 2021, he told the nation that getting a third jab "will make life easier for you in all sorts of ways." Jaw-dropping stuff from the land that gave us *Magna Carta*!

Worse still, at the time of writing, his government was planning further abominations with a so-called Consultation Document calling to replace the *HRA* with a 'Bill of Rights' that would "restore a proper balance between the rights of individuals, personal responsibility and the wider public interest."

It's not hard to see the end-game here: medical coercion as individuals are forced to take "personal responsibility" in the name of "the wider public interest."

This is not reform, as the U.K.'s so-called 'Ministry of Justice' claims, but constitutional rape.

It is also a chilling echo of the eighth principle—"Balance personal rights with social duties"—of the infamous Georgia Guidestones.[1] Completed in 1980, this monument in Elbert County, GA, called for world government and was inscribed with ten principles, beginning with, "Maintain humanity under 500,000,000 in perpetual balance with nature," a thinly veiled call for genocide.

The British government claims in its 'Consultation' that it "remains committed to the European Convention on Human Rights," but then argues in the same document that "the meaning of a right in the Bill of Rights is not necessarily the same as the meaning of a corresponding right in the European Convention on Human Rights." In short, the government gets to decide what words mean, however much we or the dictionary may beg to differ. You can see the letter I sent in rebuke to the government in Appendix VI.

Meanwhile, in collusion with Secretary of State for Justice, Dominic Raab, and Attorney General, Suella Braverman, Johnson sought an *Interpretation Bill* that would allow government ministers to overrule decisions of judges. So we see, the British government has gone full rogue.

Therefore, Messrs. Schallenberg, Mitsotakis, Macron, Johnson, and others of your ilk, we put you on notice: No matter what you enforce in your own countries, you are criminals by international definition and easily proven to be so. By persecuting a group of people based on medical status, you have committed a Crime Against Humanity under Article 7 of the **Rome Statute**, you have openly violated Articles 2 and 7 of the **UDHR**, Article 2 of the **ICESCR**, and Article 14 of the **ECHR**, and you have desecrated the Rights of the child set out in Article 2 of the **UNCRC**.

MEDICAL INCARCERATION

The vilest deeds, like poison weeds,
Bloom well in prison air.
It is only what is good in Man
That wastes and withers there.
Pale Anguish keeps the heavy gate,
And the Warder is Despair.

— OSCAR WILDE, *THE BALLAD OF*
READING GAOL

Confinement based on medical pretext began in the early days of COVID with national lockdowns, travel restrictions, and border closures throughout the world. Anxiety, loneliness, and despair set in among the imprisoned and isolated populations, while small businesses, education, and the performing arts collapsed.

No benefits were ever proven from such measures, but the costs were obvious and devastating, including surging levels of addiction, domestic abuse, suicide and, ironically, ill health from other causes left undiagnosed and untreated.

But, as if to reinforce insanity's definition as the repetition of old patterns in search of new results, authorities not only pressed on with such destructive measures but intensified them, compressing our room for movement (and for many, the room for thought) into smaller and smaller spaces. In the U.K., authorities imposed medical testing at every port, mandated filthy quarantine hotels for healthy travellers (at our own expense), and mounted all manner of bureaucratic hurdles that impeded or prevented travel abroad.

The medical discrimination was quite explicit, even on the U.K. government website which stated, "There are different rules for people who are fully vaccinated [or] not fully vaccinated." Boom, right there, blatantly flouting prohibitions against medical discrimination in the *ECHR* and Britain's own *HRA*.

Canada, with its isolation facility in Battleford, Saskatchewan, went even further under Theresa Tam, the nation's chief 'health' officer. In a 2010 documentary titled *Outbreak: Anatomy of a Plague*, she treacherously set out the tyrannical measures she seeks:

"If there are people who are non-compliant, there are definitely laws and public-health powers that can quarantine people in mandatory settings. It's potential you could track people, put bracelets on their arms, have police and other setups to ensure quarantine is undertaken. It is better to be pre-emptive and precautionary and take the heat of people thinking you might be over-reactionary, get ahead of the curve, and then think about whether you've overreacted later..."

Australia, meanwhile, with its network of COVID detention camps, border closures, and extreme police violence, has been perhaps the most zealous tyrant of all.

We have had the air sucked out of our lives. We are being suffocated, slowly, while false authority presumes to hand out tokens that will restore a little air if only we relinquish our Rights to Privacy, Travel, and bodily autonomy. It's a devilish bargain to strike, a tyrant's kiss from the likes of Boris Johnson who, shortly after the convenient emergence of the 'Omicron' variant—or rather, scariant—in December 2021, told the British population, "Get Boosted Now to protect our NHS, our freedoms and our way of life."

Easy for politicians to throw around words like "freedom" while doing exactly the opposite, demanding that we relinquish our Birthright in return for a bowl of imperial stew.[1] The bowl is poisoned, obviously, but 'old yer nose, shut yer eyes, and eat yer gruel!

Worse is planned, however, as governments build enormous internment camps in front of our noses. Private prison corporations must be salivating at the prospect of containing the medically uncooperative in Britain where, to this day, as a recent *File on 4* episode reveals, mental-health patients are imprisoned, ambushed and held down, stripped naked, and forcibly injected. The seeds of tyranny were sown in Britain long ago, and bad King John is back on the throne.

We don't have to look far to hold unlawful such measures of medical incarceration. *Magna Carta* states in Article 39,

"No free man shall be seized or imprisoned, or stripped of his rights or possessions, or outlawed or exiled, or in any way destroyed, nor will we proceed with force against him, or send others to do so, except by the lawful judgment of his peers or by the law of the land [Common Law]."

This means, as Rights advocate Andrea Tokaji points out, in a November 2021 interview with FamilyVoice Australia, "**quarantine measures can only be applied on an individual basis by a court of law.**"

Magna Carta's principle is also embodied in the **Fifth Amendment**, where none shall be "deprived of life, liberty, or property, without due process of law," and in the *Canadian Bill of Rights* (1960), which lists among fundamental freedoms "the right of the individual to life, liberty, security of the person and enjoyment of property, and the right not to be deprived thereof except by due process of law" (Part I, Section 1(a)). Nor shall legislation "authorize or effect the arbitrary detention, imprisonment or exile of any person" (Part I, Section 2(a)).

And what of property seizures in the name of public health where, as we have seen with revisions to Britain's *Public Health Act*, the government feels entitled to "seize, inspect, or destroy property"? In addition to the government's Common-Law obligations, *Magna Carta* is very clear on this in at least two articles, first in Article 39 just quoted, where none may be stripped of possessions except by the lawful judgment of his peers, and then again in Article 52: "If anyone has been dispossessed or removed by us, without the legal judgment of his peers, from his lands, castles, franchises, or from his right, we will immediately restore them to him." And again I cite the **Fifth Amendment** where "No person shall... be deprived of life, liberty, or **property**, without due process of law."

Travel Rights

> *No port is free, no place,*
> *That guard and most unusual vigilance*
> *Does not attend my taking.*

> — SHAKESPEARE, *KING LEAR*, II.III.

As Veronica notes, "Common Law provides the uninhibited Right to Travel. Actually across National

Boundaries **without the need for any kind of Passport,** as it happens."

Here, we call on *Magna Carta* again, which recognizes our Right "to **leave and return to our kingdom unharmed and without fear**" (Article 42). As the Missouri Bar website observes, the U.S. Supreme Court cited this in a 1958 case, Kent v. Dulles, "to demonstrate the ancient roots of the right to travel freely."

And this Right echoes in the *Act of Union* (1707) between England and Scotland, which states in Section IV...

"That all the Subjects of the United Kingdom of Great Britain shall from and after the Union have full Freedom and Intercourse of Trade and Navigation to and from any port or place within the said United Kingdom and the Dominions and Plantations thereunto belonging. And that there be a Communication of all other Rights Privileges and Advantages which do or may belong to the Subjects of either Kingdom..."

Then we can cite Articles 13 through 15 of the **UDHR** where everyone has freedom of movement both within a state or to leave any country and return to it. Everyone also has freedom to seek and enjoy political asylum, and to change one's nationality, and none may be arbitrarily deprived of nationality.

Similarly, the *Canadian Charter* states, under the heading 'Mobility Rights',...

"(1) Every citizen of Canada has the right to enter,
remain in and leave Canada. (2) Every citizen of Canada
and every person who has the status of a permanent
resident of Canada has the right (a) to move to and take
up residence in any province; and (b) to pursue the
gaining of a livelihood in any province" (Section 6).

Community Rights

We peoples of the so-called democracies of the West now
find ourselves being bossed about by politicians and
bureaucrats who, though they are our servants and
employees, consider themselves our masters. With a
barrage of 'mandates', they are treating our inalienable
Rights—or *un*alienable Rights if you prefer—as if they
were alienable. Other than the attacks on bodily
autonomy/medical sovereignty already discussed,
governments have tried to withhold other key Rights,
including access to education, entertainment, assembly,
and protest.

Here's a brief look at what international statute has to
say in some of these areas. The *ICESCR* upholds "the
right of everyone to education" (Article 13, Para. 1) and
to "take part in cultural life" (Article 15, Para. 1), while
the *ICCPR* recognizes "right of peaceful assembly"
(Article 21) and "the right to freedom of association with
others" (Article 22, Para. 1).

These are mirrored famously in America's **First
Amendment**: "Congress shall make no law respecting an
establishment of religion, or prohibiting the free exercise

thereof; or abridging the freedom of speech, or of the press; or the right of the people peaceably to assemble, and to petition the Government for a redress of grievances." In Britain, the *HRA* states, "Everyone has the right to freedom of peaceful assembly and to freedom of association with others" (Article 11 (1)).

PART V

THE ERA OF FALSE PROPHETS

The masses have never thirsted after truth. They turn aside from evidence that is not to their taste, preferring to deify error, if error seduce them. Whoever can supply them with illusions is easily their master; whoever attempts to destroy their illusions is always their victim.

— GUSTAVE LE BON: *THE CROWD: A STUDY OF THE POPULAR MIND*

If you have paid close attention to the 'Warp Speed' development, approval, and rollout of COVID 'vaccines', the widespread breach of scientific and medical protocols along the way, and the rush to puncture compliant or coerced bodies over every reasonable objection; if you have gasped at the orders issued by politicians, or marvelled at the coordinated messaging of governments, corporations, media, and social media, you may be wondering what dark intelligence is behind all of this. Is this just the love of money being the root of all evil, corrupting common sense and conscience? Or is there some other unseen force at work, manipulating the motivations and actions of manipulatable men and women?

Here, I will turn again to Scripture for more understanding. It really doesn't matter whether you buy into the whole Christian narrative about a fallen angel named Satan who rebelled against the Holy One, was thrown into Tartarus with his fellow conspirators, and has literally been Hell-bent on destroying God's image in Mankind ever since. None of that matters for our purposes, though you have to admit it's a great story, especially when seen through the lens of John Milton's great epic poem, *Paradise Lost*.

What *does* matter, though, is that through the character of Satan, whether regarded as an individual demon or as a metaphor for evil (in much the same way as our mythologies conjure dragons), the Bible instructs us in the stratagems now being used against us. When we understand them, we are better prepared to resist and to win our **inevitable victory** "against the authorities, against the powers of this dark world, and against the spiritual forces of evil in the heavenly realms" (*Ephesians* 6:12).

How can I be so sure this victory is inevitable? Well, I could readily draw on generalized Biblical lore, such as "Love casts out fear" (*1 John* 4:18) or "Love is stronger than death" (*Song of Solomon* 8:6). I could observe the physics of light dispelling darkness, or I could cite the Lord's words to Moses' successor, Joshua, as he prepared to attack the Amorites at Gibeon: "Do not be afraid of them; I have given them into your hand. Not one of them will be able to withstand you" (*Joshua* 10:8).

Then I could recall how the Holy One sowed confusion among the oppressors at Babel and overthrew man's arrogance (*Genesis* 11:1-9) and, crowning all, Christ's ultimate victory where, "having disarmed the powers and authorities, he made a public spectacle of them, triumphing over them by the cross" (*Colossians* 2:15).

But when it comes to the COVID story, I can be more specific by returning to the *Exodus* scene in Pharaoh's court where Aaron turns his staff into a snake. Pharaoh's sorcerers imitate the act, but Aaron's snake eats their snakes (7:10-12). Similarly, today's prophets of God are devouring the sharp-fanged creatures spawned by Pfizer and its ilk today.

What follows in the *Exodus* account? A period of struggle as the prophet brothers bring Pharaoh's kingdom to its knees. Finally, Pharaoh agrees to their demands, but then mounts a last-ditch military effort to restore the old order, culminating in his death and the demise of his army, in the Red Sea.

THAT'S HOW OUR COVID STORY ENDS TOO: WITH THE DEATHS OF PHARAOHS,

ALONG WITH THEIR EMPIRES OF SLAVERY AND MILITARISM.

Keep this ending in mind. It will sustain you when the going gets tough. The pharaohs are racing to their destruction. Deep down they know it, and they are filled with totalitarian fury because their time is short.[1]

The specific manner of their end remains to be seen. If the medical priesthood are lucky, theirs will be a quick death at the hands of mob violence as befell the false prophets of Baal after Elijah defeated them on Mount Carmel (*1 Kings 18*:40). If unlucky, they will hear their Crimes Against Humanity read out for all the world to hear before sentence is delivered.

I shudder at the prospect of seeing the perpetrators strung up and hung like butchers' carcasses, or strapped down and punctured to death with their own serums. I can't bear the idea of doing this to someone whose body was also made in the image of God, but I must admit my merciful impulses are overruled in this case. I quote again the wise words of Dave Mason, in his *Age of Prophecy* novels set in the time of Elijah. "Those who show mercy to the cruel, bring cruelty upon the merciful."

And I recall the ruthlessness Joshua instilled among his captains after they routed the five kings of the Amorites at Gibeon.

"When they had brought these kings to Joshua, he summoned all the men of Israel and said to the army commanders who had come with him, 'Come here and put your feet on the necks of these kings.' So they came forward and placed their feet on their necks. Joshua said to them, 'Do not be afraid; do not be discouraged. Be strong and courageous. This is what the Lord will do to all the enemies you are going to fight.' Then Joshua put the kings to death and exposed their bodies on five poles, and they were left hanging on the poles until evening. At sunset Joshua gave the order and they took them down from the poles and threw them into the cave where they had been hiding. At the mouth of the cave they placed large rocks, which are there to this day."

— *JOSHUA* 10:24-27

In the meantime, like Joshua, who commanded the sun to stand still over Gibeon, we will pray. How magnified are our efforts when, in faith performed and service to the Lord, we mortals reap an immortal reward. "So the sun stood still in the middle of the sky and delayed going down about a whole day. And there was never a day like it before or since, that **the Lord hearkened unto the voice of a man**" (*Joshua* 10:13-14).

THE FATHER OF LIES

Because the regime is captive to its own lies, it must falsify everything. It falsifies the past. It falsifies the present, and it falsifies the future. It falsifies statistics.

— VÁCLAV HAVEL, *THE POWER OF THE POWERLESS*

So what are we up against in the spiritual realms? We can learn much from Satan's opening scene in the New Testament, when he comes to test Jesus in the wilderness. Just as he invites Jesus to jump off the highest pinnacle of the temple (*Matthew* 4:5-7), we are invited to sacrifice our bodies to the sharpest needle, and just as he offers Jesus the kingdoms of the world "if you will bow down and worship me" (*Matthew* 4:8-9), we are promised access to the world's benefits if we will prostrate ourselves before its medical idols.

Then, as the New Testament unfolds, more patterns emerge in Satan's schemes: he is the **Father of Lies** (*John* 8:44), **Prince of the Air** (*Ephesians* 2:2), and **Accuser of the Righteous** (*Revelation* 12:10). He **masquerades as an angel of light,** and his servants masquerade as servants of righteousness (*2 Corinthians* 11:14-15), and he manipulates through **fear, greed,** and **idolatry.**

It would be impossible for one author to document the scale of deception practised on us since 'COVID' showed up in 2020, but here's a thumbnail sketch: It begins with the production of respiratory distress in residents of Wuhan, China, followed by similar symptoms showing up in other parts of the world. A devastating fear campaign ensues, with governments, media, and social-media companies concocting dread of an airborne disease. The pharmaceutical companies cash in, mounting sham vaccine trials in which they falsify data and hide the devastating injuries inflicted on trial participants. Following public rollout, they continue to conceal the ensuing mutilation and deaths, often laundering them as COVID deaths. All this is aided and abetted by captured regulatory agencies and medical journals.

Did COVID suddenly turn Big Pharma bad? No, merely made it even worse. As Russell Brand notes in a March 2021 commentary, "The transnational global megacompanies that are creating the vaccine for COVID also created the drug that led to an opioid epidemic." Front and centre in this sordid history is Johnson & Johnson which, according to an August 2019 ruling by Oklahoma judge, Thad Balkman, "lied about the science."

Exaggerating threat

And therein we find, neglected by us, the simplest, most accessible key to our liberation: a personal, non-participation in lies! Even if all is covered by lies, even if all is under their rule, let us resist in the smallest way. **Let their rule hold not through me.**

— ALEXANDER SOLZHENITSYN, *LIVE NOT BY LIES*

So how has the COVID threat been exaggerated all along? Let me count some of the ways. One dirty trick is to attribute *any* ailment, hospital admission, or death to COVID.

Here are some representative comments on a YouTube video, posted in December 2021, that illustrate the point:

"I know three people who died of cancer and one person who died in a motorcycle crash, and they put Covid on their death certificates!!! Wake up, people."

"I suffered a bilateral pulmonary embolism in April. The hospital put down it was Covid-related despite me not having any Covid in my system. Had to fight tooth and nail to get it removed from my records. Disgusting abuse of the reporting systems."

"My uncle, 90 with heart problems, died at home in March 2020, no test or symptoms, was put down as Covid death, not a heart attack. My cousin fought to have it taken off, threat of court action made doctor change death certificate."

We have also seen establishment statisticians counting admissions and deaths "with" COVID as admissions and deaths "of" or "from" COVID. Then, of course, politicians and media seize on the falsehoods to foment the fear. Sneaky stuff, isn't it?

Hiding injection injuries

You belong to your father, the devil, and you want to carry out your father's desires. He was a murderer from the beginning, not holding to the truth, for there is no truth in him. When he lies, he speaks his native language, for he is a liar and the father of lies.

— *JOHN* 8:44

And while overstating COVID damage, the authorities are desperately concealing injection damage. It began in the trials where, as we have seen, the Pfizer-induced paralysis of 12-year-old Maddie de Garay was logged as abdominal pain, and the AstraZeneca-induced devastation of Brianne Dressen was entirely omitted from results because she didn't make it to the second dose.

Meanwhile, Brook Jackson was fired from her position as a regional director of Pfizer's phase III trial in Texas on the very day she complained to the FDA about poor laboratory management, data integrity issues, and patient-safety concerns including forged signatures on informed-consent forms.

But Pfizer had been cooking the books long before COVID showed up, and its litany of medical malpractice includes kickbacks to doctors who over-prescribe.

The concealment over COVID shots continues. As Albert Benavides and others have shown, VAERS is riddled with deception, delay, and outright deletion of inconvenient truth, and fails by design. The U.S. military has also falsified vaccine-injury data for its own personnel. In Israel, meanwhile, "You have not set up an effective system for reporting side effects from the vaccines," writes Professor Qimron in his letter to the nation's Ministry of Health, cited above,

"and reports on side effects have even been deleted from your Facebook page. Doctors avoid linking side effects to the vaccine, lest you persecute them as you did with some of their colleagues. You have ignored many reports of changes in menstrual intensity and menstrual cycle times. You hid data that allows for objective and proper research (for example, you removed the data on passengers at Ben Gurion Airport). Instead, you chose to publish non-objective articles together with senior Pfizer executives on the effectiveness and safety of vaccines."

Here's more evidence from a tweet I came across on Dec. 27, 2021, one of many like it:

> "My wife had reaction and doctor and nurses in a+e said yes it was a reaction to the jab. When she saw a report a few weeks later it said dehydration."

Another tweet of the same day shows that injection deaths are being laundered as COVID deaths:

> "Just been informed by my daughter that scumbags at the hospital are trying to class her 'fully vaccinated' dad's death as a covid one because he tested positive for it after getting blood clots from the jabs. This is how the bastards are hiding jab deaths and inflating covid ones."

The murderous powers are even offering bribes to grieving relatives to falsify death records, as attested by Ernest Ramirez, another witness at Senator Ron Johnson's hearing. Ernest's only son, 16-year-old Ernesto, died from myocarditis after Pfizer's shot inflamed his heart to more than double its normal size. Interviewed by Stew Peters, Ernest recounted how the U.S. Federal Emergency Management Agency (FEMA) called and offered him money if he would remove 'enlarged heart' as the cause of death on his son's death certificate and replace it with "COVID." Ernest told FEMA he would not falsify documents for financial gain.

As encapsulated by Peters, "FEMA called you and

asked you to lie about how your son died to perpetuate a narrative, a lie, that will kill more kids." Meanwhile, Texas-based doctor, Ivan G. Melendez, who has made television appearances promoting COVID shots for children, denied Ernesto had been injected at his hospital. As Ernest told Peters,

"THESE DOCTORS ARE IN ON IT... THEY'RE ATTACKING OUR CHILDREN."

I marvel at the ingenuity of official falsehoods. Australian doctor, Peter Johnson, reports that "vaccine murders" in his country are being counted as deaths of the unvaccinated "because they define them as unvaccinated until 14 days after the jab." The same sleight of hand is at work in the Canadian province of Alberta, as reported by independent media analyst, Joel Smalley.

The medical-industrial complex must try to keep these tactics going as injection injuries mount, attributing them to the next variant of COVID, or even to another disease. Kieran Morrissey, an engineer who has worked for more than two decades at a teaching hospital in Dublin, warns the next pandemic of fear may hinge on a hitherto rare disease called 'Marburg', which presents with symptoms similar to COVID-injection injuries. Institutions aligned with Microsoft cofounder and pandemic-profiteering billionaire, Bill Gates, have already prepared for Marburg, Morrissey reports, with test kits, media scare stories falsely claiming asymptomatic spread, and a new round of emergency-use 'RiVax' shots based on the ricin toxin.

Yet another concealment strategy is the invention of a new diagnosis to mask vaccine harm. Called Post Pandemic Stress Disorder (PPSD), it could "result in a 4.5% rise in cardiovascular cases nationally," according to a British *Evening Standard article* of Dec. 14, 2021, "with those aged between 30 to 45 most at-risk." How convenient!

Amid all the mendacity, the world's power brokers can't even keep their story straight, including of course White House chief medical adviser and self-appointed high priest of 'Science', Anthony Fauci. For example, he said in August 2020 that the public "have the right to refuse a vaccine," but then called for them to be mandated for schoolteachers a year later.

The medical journals have also lined up with the vaccine establishment, as Dr Marcia Angell observes in her article, *The Faux Faith of Modern Science…*

"It is simply no longer possible to believe much of the clinical research that is published or to rely on the judgment of trusted physicians or authoritative medical guidelines. I take no pleasure in this conclusion, which I reached slowly and reluctantly over my two decades as an editor of the *New England Journal of Medicine*."

Pfizer's Abortion Jab

How dreadful it will be in those days for pregnant women and nursing mothers.

— *MATTHEW* 24:19

James A. Thorp MD is among the fiercest critics of medical tyranny, especially against pregnant women in his own field of obstetrics and gynaecology. Having reviewed the VAERS data, he reported in a December 2021 interview,

"There are more fetal deaths, fetal miscarriages, and fetal malformations that have been reported to VAERS in just six or eight months than all the other vaccinations in pregnancy in the last 32 years... And the childhood diseases I've seen, children of vaccinated moms that will be completely destroyed for their entire life. They have completely wiped out immune systems. They have chronic inflammatory diseases and autoimmune diseases, lifelong diseases."

Contrast that with an NHS press release, issued around the same time on Dec. 4, 2021, urging pregnant women to get jabbed. Among nine uses of the word 'safe' to describe the injections, it quotes then vaccines minister Maggie Throup saying, "The COVID-19 vaccines are safe and effective for pregnant women and I urge everyone to get their vaccines as soon as they can to secure this significant protection." By then, U.K. authorities had known for at least nine months that Pfizer's jab was obliterating pregnancies. We know this because Britain was the second-largest source of pregnancy data gathered in Pfizer's *Cumulative Analysis* document that tallied worldwide adverse events from its COVID injection by the end of February 2021.[1]

In this early reporting period, Pfizer recorded 270 cases where women received the jab during pregnancy. Of 27 known outcomes, including one set of twins, 26 resulted in "spontaneous abortion," and one resulted in "premature birth with neonatal death." There was but one survivor, listed as "normal outcome," among the 28 potential babies (p.12).[2]

Furthermore, if babies do somehow survive these 'transplacental' harms from their injected mothers, they are not safe from the 'transmammary harms' of tainted breast milk. The earliest VAERS reports include…

- A five-month-old boy who died after his mother got a second Pfizer dose on March 17, 2021. The next day, he "developed a rash and within 24 hours was inconsolable, refusing to eat, and developed a fever. Patient brought baby to local ER where assessments were performed, blood analysis revealed elevated liver enzymes. Infant was hospitalized but continued to decline and passed away. Diagnosis of TTP. No known allergies. No new exposures aside from the

mother's vaccination the previous day"
(VAERS ID: 1166062).

- A 16-month-old girl who developed jaundice
one day after her mother received the Johnson
& Johnson shot on Mar. 10, 2021 (VAERS ID:
1099241).
- A one-year-old boy who went into intense
febrile seizures on Feb. 19, 2021 after "vaccine
exposure via breast milk." His mother had
received a first Pfizer dose four days earlier
(VAERS ID: 1161763).
- A six-week-old boy who died on July 17, 2021
"from clots in his severely inflamed arteries," as
reported to VAERS by his 36-year-old mother.
"I had been breastfeeding my 6 week old baby
at the time that I received the first Pfizer
vaccine... I am curious if the spike protein
could have gone through the breast milk and
caused an inflammatory response in my child"
(VAERS ID: 1532154).

What motive shall we attribute to Big Pharma's
ruthless campaign of violence against children? "For
them, the younger you are, the closer you are to God, the
more pain they can inflict on God," investigative reporter
Lara Logan explained in a June 2022 interview. "So the
more you can make a baby or a small child suffer, the
greater your victory over God. And that is the only
consideration for them."

From this perspective, Pfizer is not just a corrupt

corporation counting the dollars but a rapacious priesthood counting the bodies. The younger its sacrificial victims, the greater its prestige before medical deities. What else can explain its industrial slaughter of children, not just in the cradle, but in the womb and even at the breast?

PRINCE OF THE AIR(WAVES)

I don't think I'll tune in anymore,
I don't believe in Radio 4,
It never will be the same to me...
What will I use my radio for?
I don't believe in Radio 4,
And certainly not in Radio 3.

— JAY FOREMAN, LYRICS TO SONG,
RADIO 4

How have media sources performed in sorting fact from fiction? Treacherously, diabolically, serving their corporate masters with propaganda disguised as news. And yes, I'm looking at you, Reuters, where I used to be a journalist back when you had a soul, and at you, British Broadcasting Corporation, with your manicured production line of fear, or as some aptly call you, the British Bullshit Corporation or Body Bag Corporation.[1]

Pfizer has proven especially adept at coordinating media messaging, as demonstrated by a montage of its news sponsorship that did the rounds on social media in October 2021. Meanwhile, Bill Gates has been working a more subtle version of the Pfizer playbook, giving hundreds of millions of dollars to news organizations around the world—including *The Guardian*, *Financial Times*, *Daily Telegraph*, *The Lancet*, and yes, the BBC, among a long list revealed by *MintPress*.

As Robert F. Kennedy Jr. told Jimmy Dore in their December 2021 interview, news sources "are being paid to promote pharmaceutical products, and they're doing that through direct promotion but mostly through indirect promotion by drumming up fear, by drumming up fear of infectious disease, and then telling us the only solution is vaccines."

ACCUSER OF THE RIGHTEOUS

Every genocide—whether it's Rwanda, the Holocaust—begins with 'we versus them'. So Hitler used the Jews, and later other people, as scapegoats for all that was wrong in Germany.

— SUSAN BENEDICT, *THE KILLING NURSES OF THE THIRD REICH*, 2017

With Big Pharma so embedded in Big Media, it is hardly surprising that no counternarrative is permitted, that information, perspectives, and opinions outside the official fiction are systematically silenced, and that the messengers who bring them are persecuted, prosecuted, stifled, smeared, and starved. You are likely well aware how social-media posts and even entire accounts are shut down if they don't conform. Big-Tech companies such as YouTube, Facebook, and Facebook's Instagram app are deeply saturated with government messaging, even daubing it onto individual posts, while alternative views are dispatched to oblivion with skewed search results and various bans, blocks, and deletions.

The censorship is partly enforced by Big Tech's ill-qualified and ill-informed cohort of so-called 'fact checkers', themselves financed by Big Pharma, who rig the debate, but even more insidiously by invisible 'bots' and secret equations, or 'algorithms', running in the background.

I have been on the receiving end of such censorship myself, with 'shadow-bans', strikes, and even the deletion of an entire TikTok account. Amazon.com has repeatedly blocked me from advertising some of my books on its platform, while the Canadian book retailer Kobo has outright deleted three of my books from its store altogether, including this one, on the grounds they contain 'Inappropriate content'. Meanwhile, book-promotion sites I have worked with for years are refusing to host this very book, and I am even censored from mentioning the censorship in author groups on Facebook.

Meanwhile, Internet search engines are reporting to law enforcement keywords used in searches, a blatant attack on the **First** and **Fourth Amendments** of the *Constitution.*

Such actions accord with a World Economic Forum article of April 2021 that complains "how friends fell down the wrong YouTube hole and came out speaking another language." Similarly, in a June 2021 paper, the U.N. Office of Counter-Terrorism called for 'deplatforming' "in preventing the spread of harmful narratives" and for on-line search results to be steered towards "positive, de-radicalizing content." It explicitly targets COVID 'disinformation' (intentional), 'misinformation' (unintentional), and 'mal-information' (true, but deemed harmful) that might "undermine trust in the government." Similarly, TikTok's Community Guidelines outlaw 'misinformation' that causes "the undermining of public trust in civic institutions and processes such as governments, elections, and scientific bodies."

That the medical-industrial complex feels entitled to manipulate media is obvious from an October 2020 email exchange, obtained by the American Institute for Economic Research, in which U.S. NIH director, Francis Collins, is reacting to the *Great Barrington Declaration* (GBD), a statement led by public-health scientists that warns of "the damaging physical and mental health impacts of the prevailing COVID-19 policies."

Collins tells NIAID director Fauci, "There needs to be a quick and devastating published take down of its premises. I don't see anything like that online yet. Is it underway?" In the subsequent email chain, Fauci sends back a piece from *Wired* magazine that he says "debunks this theory" and another from *The Nation*, and Collins sends Fauci a link to a *Washington Post* article opposing the *GBD*, in which Collins is quoted.

They're trying awfully hard to keep a lid on things, aren't they? As news analyst Kim Iversen observes in a December 2021 broadcast, "It was once encouraged to get a second opinion when it came to our medical care, but now, you need to go with the state-sanctioned advice, and anything other than that is a dangerous conspiracy theory."

Among the doctors and scientists standing strong against official mendacity and mandates is Dr Thorp, who described in his interview how American medical boards threatened to decertify inconvenient practitioners who speak out, meaning, "We're under a gag order." This includes the American Board of Obstetrics and Gynecology (ABOG) which in September 2021 warned members of "disciplinary actions, including suspension or revocation of their medical license" for any who provide "misinformation about the COVID-19 vaccine."

Not one to be cowered, Thorp responded,

> "You threatened me, and you threatened every other Ob/Gyn doctor—all 22,000 in the United States of America—and you have indirectly forced this vaccination on pregnant women, and there is zero safety data... You need to retract that. You need to specifically state that the vaccination should not be used in pregnancy."

The inevitable result when health-care systems are taken over by government and corporate messaging, and doctors and nurses can no longer fulfil their role as patient advocates, is a total collapse in public trust. "We've lost all of our credibility," said Thorp, "because you can't give honest, informed consent when a nurse or physician have a gag order on."

Another group targeted with censorship, smearing, and character assassination are, tragically, the injection-injured, whose cries for acknowledgement and help are not only unheard and unheeded but often met with cruelty and derision. "Vaccine-injured people are mocked; their lives have been completely destroyed," Thorp added.

> "The cartel, including the health care, the physicians, the hospitals, the three-letter agencies, the mainstream media, mock them, deride them, kick them out of the ERs, tell them they're fraudulent, take away their platforms, don't even let them tell their stories. They're banned from social media, they're banned from everything... You deride them, you mock them, you take away their voice, you throw them under the bus, and you've destroyed their lives, and you don't even give them a platform to tell their stories."

But the censorship doesn't stop there. Another class of voices that must be silenced are whistleblowers inside Big Pharma. *The Intercept* reports that Pfizer, AstraZeneca, and other large pharmaceutical corporations are trying to "block legislation that would make it easier for whistleblowers to hold companies liable for corporate fraud."

Where does all this lead? If dissenting voices are completely driven out from medicine, media, and other core institutions, there will be no more room for compassion and empathy, much less truth, and we'll be left with a hard core of compliant executioners willing to repeat the atrocities perpetrated by doctors and nurses during the Nazi era.

So let us return to our foundation of inalienable Rights. As Article 19 of the *UDHR* sets out, "Everyone has the right to freedom of opinion and expression; this right includes freedom to hold opinions without interference and to seek, receive and impart information and ideas through any media and regardless of frontiers." Freedom of Speech is also, of course, the key Right of America's **First Amendment**.

A REIGN OF FEAR

And when men are afraid, they feel safer if they can make others afraid as well—afraid of them.

— DAVE MASON, *THE LAMP OF DARKNESS*

"The perceived level of personal threat needs to be increased among those who are complacent, using hard-hitting emotional messaging." This was the advice the British government procured from its Scientific Pandemic Influenza Group on Behaviour (SPI-B) in March 2020.

Pile on the fear they did, and to devastating effect, creating a 'trauma bond' between citizen and state. Remember how fear stripped supermarket shelves in the early days of collective madness? It narrowed the field of vision to a base imperative for survival, then the fearful could be conditioned to scapegoat Rights defenders as murderers and, on the pretext of safety, to accept, welcome, and even call for tyrannical measures against them. So much for "love your neighbour as yourself." As Dr Dhand warns in a December 2021 broadcast, "Human beings are capable of all kinds of madness once they have been infected with fear."

And what happens when awareness spreads among the vaccinated that they may have been mutilated? Some will reach across the vaccine divide to find kinship and healing with the unvaccinated, realizing that both groups have a common enemy in the 'frog' oligarchs, but others will lash out in anger at the easiest target, the nearest unjabbed person, and find some temporary relief if others can be forced into the same sinking boat.

It won't be rational, but what is rational when fear and anger reign? Still, under international medical codes, none should know the medical status of another in the first place!

Fear, rather than hate, is perhaps the most fitting antonym for love in these times. Fear shuts down thought, stifles the spirit of enquiry, and divides people who would otherwise have no quarrel. As Laura Dodsworth notes in *A State of Fear: How the UK government weaponised fear during the Covid-19 pandemic*, "We were the most frightened population in the world" after COVID's purported arrival in 2020. She attributes this to the British government's relentless campaign, informed by behavioural scientists on the payroll, and with the connivance of media and especially the BBC, to intensify the sense of threat among the population.

These behavioural scientists are using 'nudge' tactics,

according to Dodsworth, meaning the use of psychological drivers beneath surface awareness to "change your thinking and behaviour without you even being aware of it." Britain, she reports, is a pioneer in nudge theory and has operated a 'Nudge Unit', officially known as The Behavioural Insights Team (BIT), since 2010.

> "Britain is so good at behavioural insights that we export it all over the world. The Nudge Unit is now a profit-making 'social purpose limited company' with offices in London, Manchester, Paris, New York, Singapore, Sydney, Wellington, and Toronto. It has run more than 750 projects, and in 2019 alone worked in 31 countries."

Isn't it remarkable that the cities listed happen to be in the nations spearheading COVID authoritarianism?! It seems that our great British ingenuity that cracked the Enigma Code during the Second World War has now been weaponized against the home population to crack the psyche and break the will. What a tragedy that the British boffin has become an operative in Satan's workshop!

What's more, this boffin is marching in lockstep with, rather than opposing, counterparts at Germany's Ministry of the Interior who are doing the same or even worse. Dodsworth quotes a *Welt am Sonntag* article showing German scientists sought to create a 'shock effect' on their population to lay the groundwork for 'measures of a preventive and repressive nature.' "The German government, and the scientists it employed, collaborated to bring images of people choking to death at home, and to inflict fear and guilt on children, in order to make the population follow rules for an epidemic which had been deliberately exaggerated."

And Satan's workshop continues to recruit. "In the autumn of 2020," Dodsworth observes, "I notice 10 new behavioural science roles advertised in the NHS and Public Health England." The Nudge Unit even attempted to recruit her too. At least ten government departments now deploy behavioural insights teams, she writes, including one at the Home Office that "attempts to covertly engineer the thoughts of people."

And all this for a purported disease called 'COVID', which Public Health England downgraded from a 'High consequence infectious disease (HCID)' on Mar. 19, 2020 (yes 2020, not 2021), where it had briefly sat alongside Ebola.

Is it not the job of statesmen to see a bigger picture than the hired nerds of any field? If they did not, then John F. Kennedy might have been persuaded to "fry" Cuba with nuclear weapons in 1962, as advised by his Air Force Chief of Staff, Curtis LeMay, during the Cuban missile crisis. Enlightened leaders would dismiss the dystopian dreams of behavioural scientists—dismiss them from government altogether—in favour of common sense and a long-term view.

But not this lot. The British government, armed with a compliant BBC, have pursued the fear narrative with a maniacal zeal that even chief Nazi propagandist Joseph

Goebbels would admire. When one disease 'variant' has exhausted its shock value, the government conjures another, such as 'Omicron'. It exhibits all the ferocity of a common cold but as, in BBC parlance, it "ripped through" the population, Boris Johnson raised the 'Covid Alert level' to its second highest level of '4' and warned the nation in a Dec. 12, 2021 speech, "Do not make the mistake of thinking Omicron can't hurt you; can't make you and your loved ones seriously ill."

All to persuade citizens to take a third dose of Big Pharma's serum:

> "A wave of Omicron through a population that was not boosted would risk a level of hospitalisation that could overwhelm our NHS and lead sadly to very many deaths. So we must act now. Today we are launching the Omicron Emergency Boost, a national mission unlike anything we have done before in the vaccination programme to Get Boosted Now."

I counted the number of times Johnson said "booster", "boostered", or "boost" in this short speech—18! It's one of those words that sounds weirder, the more you say it. The speech might make for a fun drinking game, but it's no basis for public-health policy.

As Dodsworth saw and foresaw in *A State of Fear*, "A government could keep new variant bait and switch policies going for as long as there are viruses. That's forever, by the way."

But politicians will end up blowing on dying coals as

fear fatigue sets in. The public are getting ever more weary of the propaganda and tune it out as more and more people realize we've witnessed a well orchestrated fiction, its methodology akin to the light shows of different colours used to depict varying levels of terrorism threat. It's a smoke-and-mirrors magic show engineered to keep the population on edge and primed to accept even more Government interference and control in their lives. Yet the measures imposed on the basis of this fiction are very real and injurious, destroying lives, livelihoods, and the very fabric of society.

And what about the trauma inflicted on children? I quoted Britain's **Serious Crime Act** before. Let's take another look now, for its definition of cruelty against children includes "**psychological suffering or injury as well as physical harm.**" Has any child in the U.K. been left psychologically unharmed by the government's blitz of fear, shaming, lies, and threats?

Has any adult for that matter? Quite apart from all the physical violations of the **Hippocratic Oath** now underway, what about the psychological ones? Are they not Crimes Against Humanity too? Article 6 of the **Rome Statute** says they are! Acts "causing serious bodily **or mental harm** to members of the group" are listed there as a form of 'Genocide'.

As Dodsworth writes, "the government weaponised our fear against us." Yes, we have been psychologically tortured.

Furthermore, when Government and Media incite us to turn against each other, isn't that also a Crime Against

Humanity? Remember the headlines I quoted in the Introduction? "The unvaccinated are putting us all at risk." "I'm Furious at the Unvaccinated." "It is only a matter of time before we turn on the unvaccinated." As Article 25 of the **Rome Statute** points out, anyone who "publicly incites others to commit genocide" is also criminally liable.

Why hasn't there been more resistance from Parliament? I find it hard to fathom. And why has Britain's so-called Opposition, the Labour Party, completely rolled over? What bribes or threats are in play? What secret-society oaths? And what blackmailing material—or 'kompromat'—is ready to be unleashed against any who dares call out the murderous agenda of autocrats?

But let us also read between the lines of Johnson's Omicron scare speech to see where the threat *really* lies. "We will also assist this emergency operation," he said, "by deploying 42 military planning teams across every region... and training thousands more volunteer vaccinators." This is where things get really chilling for those who see through the façade. With thousands more hastily assembled skin-piercers roaming the land with military support, yet clueless about **Nuremberg, Helsinki,** or the **UDBHR**, Britain is cooking up a kind of tyranny we've never seen before.

THE LOVE OF MONEY

Though I travel to the ends of the earth, I find the same accursed system -- I find that all the fair and noble impulses of humanity, the dreams of poets and the agonies of martyrs, are shackled and bound in the service of organized and predatory Greed!

— UPTON SINCLAIR, *THE JUNGLE* (1906)

The lubrication for all the demonic tactics we have seen is, of course, the love of money. And there is an awful lot of it at stake. The People's Vaccine Alliance reports profits from COVID injections spawned nine new billionaires and that the pharmaceutical enterprises took $34 billion in profits—profits, not revenue—in 2021.

We need look no further than Anthony Fauci to see the financial ties linking corporations, governments, bureaucrats, politicians, and media in unholy alliance. As Robert F. Kennedy Jr. told Jimmy Dore, Fauci "walks those drugs through the FDA approval process which he completely controls from the bottom up, and then he gets them approved, and then in many cases he himself profits." In the case of Moderna, "His agency owns half of that vaccine, and they stand to make billions of dollars."

Financial ties also quickly snuffed out altruistic impulse when the Bill & Melinda Gates Foundation persuaded Britain's Oxford University, a major beneficiary, to change its vaccine distribution model from an open-licence, royalty-free platform available for any manufacturer, to an exclusive license controlled by AstraZeneca. Gates, who has a long history of collaboration with Fauci, is also a leading funder of the World Health Organization through his foundation.

The medical-industrial complex has also been helping itself liberally to the public purses of our nations, including Canada, where the government refuses to account for CA$240 billion it dispensed in COVID-19 aid, though we do know some of it went to bribing media outlets.

In America, meanwhile, public money is used to incentivize hospital deaths. In a January 2022 interview, Truth for Health Foundation president, Elizabeth Vliet MD, explains that the U.S. government is running "a bounty on people's lives" by paying hospitals per positive COVID test, per patient put on a ventilator, and for each death attributed to COVID.

Rights attorney, Leigh Dundas, calls this a 'murder-for-hire scheme'. Speaking at a January 2022 conference, she said of Fauci, "You are the new Josef Mengele, and we are living through another genocide or holocaust, and the hospitals have become the new ovens of Auschwitz."

What other financial ties do we see? Too many to mention, but a representative sample includes White House adviser Anita Dunn, whose consulting firm represents Pfizer; Biden's domestic policy adviser, Susan Rice, who holds up to $5 million in Johnson & Johnson; and White House science adviser Eric Lander, who has up to a million dollars in shares of Pfizer partner, BioNTech. Many in Biden's inner circle also have links to consulting firm Albright Stonebridge Group, which has represented Pfizer.

As former professional mountain-bike champion Kyle Warner came to realize, after Pfizer's product "broke my heart literally and figuratively" and put a stop to his career, "There is a party in this situation that's making tens of billions of dollars from this situation. They're operating with immunity, they're also responsible for a lot of the scientific data and clinical trials being pushed through, and they also sponsor a lot of the mainstream-media narrative."

Are things any better in the U.K.? The Medicines and Healthcare products Regulatory Agency (MHRA) also receives funding from Gates, and the new BBC chairman, Richard Sharp, has donated over £400,000 to the ruling Conservative Party. Also, as *The Guardian* reported (drawing on the little integrity it had left), drug companies are secretly lining the pockets of British members of Parliament.

Following the money in all this reveals a similar

mechanism for COVID profiteering as that described by Julian Assange in 2011 for the West's invasion and decades-long occupation of Afghanistan. There, the aim was to wash money out of national tax bases and into the hands of the military-industrial complex. Now, it's the *medical*-industrial complex that's rejoicing!

I close this section by saying I could never understand the ignorant faith so many people, including many of my friends, put in Big Pharma's products. Had they taken even a cursory look at the fraud and corruption at the root, they would surely have inferred corrupt products would be the fruit.

THE RISE AND FALL OF IDOLATRY

The state takes the place of God,... and State slavery is a form of worship.

— CARL JUNG, *THE UNDISCOVERED SELF*

By now, you are aware that the COVID response has awakened monsters among us, that we are witnessing a phenomenon far beyond the commonplace fraud, corruption, and greed that have always greased the wheels of Government. There is something utterly demonic at work here. A cult has taken control in this time of revived idolatry, a cult of service to false gods and medical deities who demand our obedience, our sacrifice, our perpetual tithes and enslavement, while offering us nothing but poison in return, all to achieve some ghastly final solution.

In the words of astrologer Sarah Varcas,...

"The new religion of Covid, which tolerates no debate, no question, no doubt, has spread its reign of terror across the globe whilst those who struggle to preserve the most basic human rights and retain some semblance of a life worth living – an independent livelihood, the right to make personal health choices free of state and societal coercion, a nurturing social network of real-life human connection – they are vilified and silenced. Independent, nuanced thought is now a crime in a world where propaganda rules, and facts are sacrificed on the altar of mob-rule and the tyranny of fear."[1]

Big Pharma has done all this in the name of 'Science' but, as Dr Dhand points out in his December 2021 broadcast, "When you're no longer allowed to ask reasonable, proper questions, you're no longer in the realm of science, you're in the realm of something akin to religious extremism."

It conjures the nightmare image of Fauci and Gates officiating at some unholy communion where supplicants are called forth to the altar, bend the knee, and drink from a poisoned chalice while, from twisted pipes, discordant sounds swell from an infernal organ.

The sacrificial child is brought forth, masked and muted, trembling, his eyes wide with fear. Deaf to his muffled screams, they force him onto the altar while his proud parents, honoured guests of the assembly, look on with stoic resolution.

Perhaps there is a hint of a tear in the mother's eye, a twitch of the father's lip, but when the boy's eyes appeal to theirs, he sees no light in them. He struggles, squeals, and writhes, but the cheers of the crowd drown out his cries. Fauci's cardinals hold him down. Lifting the sacred needle, the high priest proclaims:

"To the one who gave us Pfizer and Moderna, to the bringer of the miracle cure, the saviour of humanity, and to the one who sent his servants Johnson & Johnson and AstraZeneca, receive thou this offering that we, thy devoted and worshipful acolytes, may receive great abundance."

And as the cold steel pierces the tender flesh of the child, there is great jubilation among the assembly.

For, in these evil days, children are being lined up as sacrificial lambs, Molech is ascendant, and now, instead of provoking the outrage that followed his child rapes in the Catholic Church, he is winning applause for his predations.

> *An evil soul producing holy witness*
> *Is like a villain with a smiling cheek,*
> *A goodly apple rotten at the heart :*
> *O, what a godly outside falsehood hath.*

> — SHAKESPEARE, *THE MERCHANT OF*
> *VENICE*, I.III

For Molech, too, masquerades as an angel of light, while his accomplice Pfizer is "playing Messiah," to quote WION broadcast host Palki Sharma in a Feb. 24, 2021 broadcast. Meanwhile, Satan's servants, themselves masquerading as servants of righteousness (2 *Corinthians* 11:15), are drunk on their new-found power. They presume, for example, to tell nurses if they may receive 'religious exemptions' from medical mandates when "No" is, was, and always will be, exemption enough.

They are, of course, oblivious to Article 18 of the *ICCPR*: "No one shall be subject to coercion which would impair his freedom to have or to adopt a religion or belief of his choice" (Para. 2). As set out in Appendix IV of this book, a letter intended for 'religious-exemption' hearings, no individual or committee gets to play God and say who will ascend to Heaven or who descend (*Romans* 10:6-7). That kind of presumption is about as Satanic as it gets!

> You said in your heart,
> "I will ascend to the heavens;
> I will raise my throne
> Above the stars of God;
> I will sit enthroned on the mount of assembly,
> On the utmost heights of Mount Zaphon.
> I will ascend above the tops of the clouds;
> I will make myself like the Most High."
> But you are brought down to the realm of the dead,
> To the depths of the pit.
>
> — *ISAIAH* 14:13-15

But the favoured ones, the virtue signallers, the self-righteous who masquerade (and mask-erade) as servants of righteousness, bring their servile sacrifices to the state altar. To paraphrase Christ's tirade against the pharisees in *Matthew* 23, they are a brood of vipers, venomous in their denouncements, and poised to strike at any heretic. They strain out gnats in the lives of others but swallow the camel of genocide themselves, and though exalted in their own eyes and in the eyes of the totalitarian state, they are but whitewashed tombs, clad with worldly respectability but filled with the bones of the dead and everything unclean.

"In the totalitarian religion," explains Academy of Ideas in a January 2022 essay, "there are the chosen people, and there are the sinners. The chosen ones... are the pious who follow the state's commands with unquestioning obedience. The sinners are the non-believers, the heretics who stand in the way of the so-called greater good and prevent the forward march of history."

Thus, every voice of moderation is driven from the unholy orders until only the extremists are left. For example, in August 2021, Dr Marion Gruber resigned in protest as director of the FDA's Office of Vaccines Research and Review because the Biden administration rolled out booster shots before officials had a chance to review them. Her deputy, Dr Philip Krause, also resigned.

"The social transformation that unfolds under totalitarianism is built upon, and sustained by delusions," the Academy of Ideas observes in another essay, "for only deluded men and women regress to the child-like status of obedient and submissive subjects and hand over complete control of their lives to politicians and bureaucrats. Only a deluded ruling class will believe that they possess the knowledge, wisdom, and acumen to completely control society in a top-down manner, and only when under the spell of delusions would anyone believe that a society composed of power-hungry rulers on the one hand, and a psychologically regressed population on the other, will lead to anything other than mass suffering and social ruin."

Are these the end-times foreseen in *Revelation* 18:23? "By thy sorceries were all nations deceived" is the *King James Version*. "By your magic spell, all the nations were led astray" is the *New International Version*.

In the original Greek, the sentence is "ὅτι ἐν τῇ φαρμακείᾳ σου ἐπλανήθησαν πάντα τὰ ἔθνη," in which the word used for 'sorceries' or 'magic spell' is 'φαρμακεια', 'pharmakeia'. Ring any bells? As explained more fully in the Non Toxic Home blog, the term means 'potion', 'poison', 'medicine', 'drug', or 'spell'.

Well then, since we are in a spiritual battle, let us draw inspiration from the Old-Testament prophets who railed against the idolatry of political leaders... and killed them! Yes, Moses killed Pharaoh and his army, and Elijah killed Ahab and Jezebel and their son Ahaziah, and oh yes, 450 false prophets and a hundred men at arms. Not with the weapons of the world, but by the Word of God.

Elijah's victory over the establishment priests is one

of the crowning moments of Bible history and, like the snake battle in Pharaoh's court, offers compelling prophecy as to how the COVID story will play out. He challenges the corrupt priesthood to a contest on Mount Carmel. They are to build an altar and call on their god Baal to send down fire upon it. Then Elijah will build an altar of his own and call on the Lord to send down fire. "The god who sends down fire, is god" (*1 Kings* 18:24).

Elijah's opponents fail in their call to Baal, though they cut their own flesh to ribbons in the attempt, but Elijah spectacularly succeeds, after which he orders the people to seize his opponents and let none escape. A massacre ensues, filling the Kishon Valley with blood.

Clearly, the people of Israel were seething with rage for all they and their kin had suffered from this cult, and the mob justice they delivered was swift and merciless.

Imagine, then, the fury that will be unleashed when Justice befalls this current crop of miscreants who, worse than cutting their *own* flesh, sought to cut *ours*, and that of our children, and to profit from it, who imposed locked-down misery and incarceration on the people while they partied in high places. What revenge will be exacted for the elderly parents who died alone in care homes, for the lives lost to addiction and suicide, the ruined livelihoods, murdered businesses, and shattered dreams?

And what price shall be demanded for loved ones injured, crippled, or killed by injection, for children sacrificed, athletes maimed, musicians silenced, and a generation traumatised for life? And all to make the obscenely rich even richer and their middle-class functionaries a little more comfortable, while the public purse was looted to fill the coffers of ministers' friends.

WITH SO MUCH BLOOD CRYING OUT FROM THE GROUND, WHAT COURT COULD DISPENSE JUSTICE FOR ALL OF THAT?!

THE NEPHILIM DESCENDANTS

Truth is stranger than fiction, it is said. And, as Shakespeare reminds us, "There are more things in Heaven and Earth, Horatio/ Than are dreamt of in your philosophy" (*Hamlet*, I.v). Therefore, until the hidden is made known (*Luke* 8:17) and prophecies cease (*1 Corinthians* 13:9-10), permit me to talk of things unseen as well as seen.

The first recorded attempt to defile our genetic inheritance is described in *Genesis* 6:4: "The sons of God went to the daughters of men and had children by them. They were the heroes of old, men of renown."

With words like 'hero' and 'renown', it makes this hybrid race — part angel and part human, and known as the 'Nephilim' — sound somehow noble and virtuous, but what if the passage were instead rendered, "Rebellious angels raped women, and their resultant offspring grew up to be murderous bandits, men of ill repute."

Going by the excellent analysis of author Ryan Pitterson, in his 'Beginning and End' podcast series on the Nephilim, the latter seems more accurate. For Satan knew, as decreed in *Genesis* 3:15, that a descendant of the woman would arise to destroy him, and therefore initiated this defilement of the daughters of Eve as a "large scale, widespread assault on human DNA, to make humanity something other than image-bearers of God and by doing this, potentially corrupting the lineage that would lead to the Messiah."

Though these Nephilim were wiped out by the Flood, a trace may have persisted through the wife of Noah's son, Ham. This mutant race were a "wicked demon brood," in the words of third-century theologian, Tertullian (c. 155-240 AD), whose "great business is the ruin of mankind."

Could this demon-infused bloodline explain the resurgence of the psychopath in our age, someone who can kill without remorse, someone who shares not our natural instinct to love others as we love ourselves? When we witness people behaving with unspeakable cruelty, we may say, "They have a screw loose," but could that loose screw be the genetic disposition of a Nephilim descendant?

If Satan's idea was to corrupt God's image in Mankind by hybridizing our race, and the Flood set him back, wouldn't he try again? It's a question worth considering in light of Pfizer CEO Albert Bourla's boast, in a November 2021 interview, that mRNA injections—the technology used in COVID 'vaccines'—are a doorway to 'gene editing'. What mythical beast would he have in mind?

PART VI

A NEW EARTH

A more unequal match can hardly be.
Christian must fight an angel, but you see
The valiant man by handling sword and shield
Doth make him, though a dragon, quit the field.

— JOHN BUNYAN, *THE PILGRIM'S*
PROGRESS

The bewildering pace of authoritarianism in recent years has put us on the back foot, scrambling to make sense of it all. That seems part of the plan, to knock us out before we realize what hit us, a cynical replay of the 'Shock and Awe' strategy the U.S. military rained down on the people of Iraq in 2003.

But what happens when the autocrats have played their last hand? There will be a great and mighty reckoning that not only overthrows them but the system that spawned them. Each member of the oppressors' network, at every level of command, will find nowhere to hide. There will be no place of refuge from a people ready to assert their Birthright and to abolish forms of Government that were destructive of the Life, Liberty, and Pursuit of Happiness championed in the *Declaration of Independence*.

A similar outcome is foreseen in **Magna Carta** where, in Article 61, if the governing power "offend in any respect against any man" and redress is not given within 40 days, we may "assail" it "in every way possible, with the support of the whole community of the land" and seize any of its lands, buildings, or property (Article 61).

Will it involve violence, which I understand in the narrow sense of conventional violence to people? I have no moral argument to offer here, only a practical one, that the state is better funded and equipped than we are. If we are playing to our strengths, it's not our best option. We also have Christ's admonition that those who live by the sword will die by the sword (*Luke* 22:36). However, if police forces and military are true to their oaths, defend fundamental Rights, and defy dictatorship, some righteous violence may unfold.

In any case, prophets have greater forces at our disposal than mere weaponry. Moses wielded plague and wiped out an army, Elijah killed the entire house of Ahab and all the false prophets of Baal, slew Queen Jezebel with a prophet's decree, and called down fire from the sky to destroy two detachments of soldiers (2 *Kings* 1:9-12).

His successor, Elisha, blinded enemy soldiers, unleashed panic among a besieging army, and thwarted every ambush attempted by invaders, all without lifting a sword (*2 Kings* 6-7).

> "The man of God sent word to the king of Israel: 'Beware of passing that place, because the Arameans are going down there.' So the king of Israel checked on the place indicated by the man of God. Time and again Elisha warned the king, so that he was on his guard in such places. This enraged the king of Aram. He summoned his officers and demanded of them, 'Tell me! Which of us is on the side of the king of Israel?' 'None of us, my lord the king,' said one of his officers, 'but Elisha, the prophet who is in Israel, tells the king of Israel the very words you speak in your bedroom.' "
>
> — *2 KINGS* 6:9-12

For other parallels to our story's conclusion, see *Exodus* 7:12, 14:28, *1 Kings* 18:40, 22:37-38, *2 Kings* 1, 9:32-33, and *Esther* 7:9-10.

Then, instead of us trembling before governments, they shall tremble before us, wondering what horror shall befall them if they cross the elect and trigger our prophets' curses. Quoting from my epic poem, *Elijah,*...

For what can armour, helmet, sword, or shield
In that arena do where prophets wield
Their power, and works of angels are unsealed?
This is a battle of another field.

But I am not defining property damage as violence. If any property or infrastructure serves the tyrants and corporate aggressors, or funnels the flow of corrupt funds or serums, then it is fair game. Its destruction and sabotage are holy and righteous acts, akin to Christ's zeal when he overturned corrupt tables in his father's house (*Mark* 11:15-16).

THE TIME OF TRUE PROPHETS

And when he has tried me, I shall come forth as gold.

— *JOB* 23:10

Of course, the oppressors will not hesitate to wield violence themselves, for violence is their native language. They even paint their response to COVID in the language of war, though an alleged virus can be no more injured by their weaponry than water stabbed with a knife, nor visible to their surveillance than a fart in the wind.

In H.G. Wells' novel, *The War of the Worlds*, it is a pathogen that saves the people of Earth from alien invaders who sought to wipe them out or enslave them. (Excuse the plot spoiler if you didn't know.) Well, we have had our sovereignty invaded too, and by creatures who in their behaviour and demeanour are no longer recognizable as our own species, aliens who would alienate us from the inalienable.

But it won't work. I guarantee you. In the end, it won't work. Their end shall be what their deeds deserve. Moreover, we have unseen allies fighting alongside us.

"When the servant of the man of God got up and went out early the next morning, an army with horses and chariots had surrounded the city. 'Oh no, my lord! What shall we do?' the servant asked. 'Don't be afraid,' the prophet answered. 'Those who are with us are more than those who are with them.' And Elisha prayed, 'Open his eyes, Lord, so that he may see.' Then the Lord opened the servant's eyes, and he looked and saw the hills full of horses and chariots of fire all around Elisha. As the enemy came down toward him, Elisha prayed to the Lord, 'Strike this army with blindness.' So he struck them with blindness, as Elisha had asked."

— *2 KINGS* 6:15-18

Therefore, as fear is assuaged when barriers of perception are removed, let us pray to receive that sight with which Elisha and his servant were gifted.

Our revolution will also move in prophetic prayer, wielding intercessory 'keys' in Heaven that open and close things on Earth. "Truly, I say to you, whatever you bind on Earth shall be bound in Heaven, and whatever you loose on Earth shall be loosed in Heaven" (*Matthew* 16:19).

So take your stand before the throne of the Most High and claim the keys that shut down the toxic flows of funds and serums, that unlock the bank vaults of tyrants and spill their contents to the poor and hungry. Murderous weapons we destroy, broken bodies we mend, rulers seated on high we topple from their already tilting thrones.

As exemplified in the lives of Moses and Elijah, we call down Heaven's intervention in the overthrow of leaders and their functionaries. Moses did according to the word of God in his dealings with Pharaoh, but the Lord also did according to the word of Moses (*Exodus* 8:13,31). As Dave Mason reminds us, in his aforementioned *Age of Prophecy* novels, "What the righteous decree, the Holy One carries out."

And that status of righteousness is not because we've had a good life or done the right things. It is a gift conferred on us from above. Listen to the testimony of John Bunyan:

"But one day, as I was passing in the field, and that too with some dashes of conscience, fearing lest all was not right, suddenly this sentence fell upon my soul, Thy righteousness is in Heaven; and methought withal, I saw, with the eyes of my soul, Jesus Christ at God's right hand; there, I say, is my righteousness; so that wherever I was, or whatever I was a-doing, God could not say of me, he lacks my righteousness, for that was just before him. I also saw, moreover, that it was not my good frame of heart that made my righteousness better, nor yet my bad frame of heart that made my righteousness worse; for my righteousness was Jesus Christ himself, the same yesterday, and today, and for ever (*Hebrews* 13:8)."[1]

Bunyan understood that, as a member of the body of Christ, he was "flesh of his flesh, and bone of his bone" and that, "if he and I were one, then his righteousness was mine, his merits mine, his victory also mine." Bunyan could imagine God saying, "Behold! My son is by me, and upon him I look, and will deal with thee according as I am pleased with him."

Yes, God will deal with me and you according as he is pleased with Christ. Therefore, doubt not your worthiness to carry the divine flame, to be the Lord's messenger of holy Rights declarations. You are clothed in him, and all his merits are yours! And if you ever *do* doubt your fitness for the task, lean on *his* immortal worthiness instead.

Nor do not worry when oil- and stock-markets appear eternally bullish, when billionaires make a killing literally and metaphorically, and the deities of 'pharmakeia' glean extortionate and extortioned profits, nor that the forces of authoritarianism appear to be winning. These are but temporary trends. Moses didn't bring down Pharaoh overnight; it took a sustained campaign in which Egypt cajoled and threatened, relented and reversed, bargained and broke its promises. We know how earthly power works.

But the autocrats' ball is over, the writing's on the wall, their downfall is inevitable. We are not fighting this battle alone, equipped only with a mortal's instruments of hand and voice, though these are powerful in themselves, but with decrees of divine enforcement!

CASTING OUT FEAR

We don't do fear as followers of the Lord Jesus.

— MARK GORING, CANADIAN
CATHOLIC PRIEST

Stories need villains. Our modern myths testify to this. Who would Harry Potter be without Voldemort; Batman without Joker; or Luke Skywalker without Darth Vader? Now, with so many villains at large, we have a target-rich training ground for honing our tyrant-slaying skills. These include the utterance of Rights declarations, knowing that when we do so, we invoke the Creator's authority...

He does as he pleases
With the powers of Heaven

And the peoples of the Earth.
No one can hold back his hand
Or say to him: 'What have you done?'

— DANIEL 4:35

Most in the magical community of Harry Potter's world would not speak the name, Voldemort, instead referring to him as "he who must not be named." Some realities seem too horrific to face, which was my experience in hearing British funeral director John O'Looney, a man who works at the coal-face of life and death, bear witness both to the genocide already unleashed by the British government—with the NHS as its accomplice—and to even worse planned.

It's terrifying stuff, worse than any horror film I have seen or Hollywood could imagine, not for solo viewing perhaps, and certainly not before bedtime. It put me in a fever of fear, but it also made me more aware of the devil's schemes (2 *Corinthians* 2:11) and, after the fever passed, more immune to another onslaught.

O'Looney says in the interview, "I'm not frightened of dying. I'm frightened of living like this." Well, I *am* frightened of dying, but would still choose death over a life enslaved. If we are facing a genocidal cult—and it appears that we are—then we are all targeted already. Better to be targeted for expressing our views than anonymously crushed under the wheels of an imperial juggernaut.

With Christians the world over, I yearn for Jesus' return now more than ever. May it be soon, O Lord, for your people are sore distressed. I feel overmatched by an enemy who is relentless and seems unstoppable. I am even tempted in moments of weakness to ascribe to this enemy the omniscience and omnipotence that are only yours!

Yet I remind myself and the Reader that he who is in us is greater than he who is in them (*1 John* 4:4). I have never been keen on "us and them" language before but it fits now, and it has nothing to do with medical status. The 'us' are we who always wanted to be left alone to get on with our lives, and the 'they' are those who want to imprison us, enslave us, torture us, rape, maim, mutilate, and murder us, and even tear out our hearts. 'THEY' are "The Hierarchy Exploiting You" (I forget who coined this acronym.) We therefore claim in Heaven, that they are bestowed on Earth, the protections of *Psalm* 91, not just from "the pestilence that stalks in the darkness" but also from "the arrow that flies by day."

What antidotes are there to fear? One is to realize that fear fantasies are not prophecies. How many of us have taken flights and imagined the plane falling from the sky, or swum in the sea and imagined a shark attack? I gather too from a friend more experienced in this, that the kind of fear fever I went through is something of a rite of passage in this arena.

I also contextualize fear with the help of Shakespeare's famed lines in *As You Like It*...

All the world's a stage
And all the men and women merely players.
They have their exits and their entrances...

Consider the actor playing Hamlet. His character enters in Act I and exits after Hamlet's death in Act V, but the actor himself does not die. His simultaneous offstage life is untouched by the Danish court and its deadly politics.

In the same way, we actors, clothed in mortal skin to play a role on the world's stage, have a greater life and existence off-world, outliving our exit and preceding our entrance. This greater life is untouched by the make-believe, the theatre of this world. What's more, we have a direct line to the Playwright who made this stage, and we may call on him to write new scenes, summon new allies, shine new lights, and even to change the plot. Quoting again from my epic poem, *Elijah*,...

How false our fears may be, whether in thought
Or dream, and do they not often precede,
As in this case, fulfilment of hopes sought?
Fears tempt us to inaction, to concede,
Or test if we are resolute in deed
To see through phantom menaces, transcend
Illusory distractions, reach our end.

There's a physical metaphor we can invoke too, called The Unbendable Arm Exercise, which I learned from soul teacher, Darren Eden: Make a fist and crook your arm, with elbow by your side, so that your forearm is parallel to the floor, knuckles facing downward. Ask a friend to try and push your fist up to your shoulder, and try to resist them. Now do the same again, but instead of trying to resist them, pick a point on the wall and imagine a beam of light going from your fist to that point. Your arm becomes unbendable!

What does this mean in an era of dictatorship? That when we gaze upon the object of our love—love of constitution, love of God's image in Man, reverence for our ancestors who loved us so much that they wrote these declarations to protect us—then the fears that seek to bend us are rendered powerless.

I recall the wise words of the late Vladimir Zelenko MD, the much maligned doctor who was among the first to see through, and call out, the 'COVID' deceptions…

"Each human-being is being given a choice right now. The choice is: 'Do I give into the fear or not?' And you have to have a mechanism in place to deal with the fear. Otherwise, it overtakes you. So for some people it's faith. For me, it's faith. So if I ever find myself in a fear state, I realize that **anxiety can only live in the psychological space where God is absent.** So if I fill the void with the consciousness of the divine, and that suppresses my anxiety, what I've done is taken that potentially negative event and I've used it as a motivation for spiritual growth. And that's one choice. The other is, you get into the fear and it causes you to go down the slippery slope of psychological co-dependence on human beings and on vaccines and on the whims of man. And it's obvious to me which will have a better outcome."

I remember, too, that the devil must flee from us when we resist him (*James* 4:7)—now, that's a statement we may call 'Law'—and that we have authority to overcome all the power of the enemy (*Luke* 10:19).

Above all, love casts out fear, and love is stronger than death. We love our inalienable Rights, and we love the immortal documents on which they are written. Even if we walk through the Valley of the Shadow of Death, the Lord is obliged by his own promises to uphold us as we uphold this love.

"If you follow your conscience, that stops the devil in his tracks, because he doesn't know how to handle it," attests former Salt Lake City police officer, Eric Moutsos, in a December 2021 interview on the Sheriff Mack Show. "He doesn't have authority over you when you follow your God-given conscience. *God* has authority over you when you follow what's inside of your heart."

And if Satan has no authority over us, much less do his lackeys. When we stand in the authority of Christ and say, "I do not consent," we wield an otherworldly power against Satan and his operatives. As the *Strawman* documentary reminds us, "They always need your consent, and this is where your power really lies. With knowledge always comes power—the power not to fear, the power to take a stand against anyone or any corporation that threatens you, the power to say No."

Moutsos acknowledges this is the 'narrow path' (*Matthew* 7:14)...

"You need to follow your conscience because that is the light of Christ inside of you, that is the Word of God inside of you. And if you do that, it's going to be hard. God never says it's going to be easy. That road, when you follow your conscience, that's going to be a lonely road. But that's the whole test, that's the whole reason why we're here on Earth."

Though our faith is under assault like never before,...

"God will have your back. He's bound. That's a gift. He wants to bless us. He wants to show us, he wants to prove that he's the one in charge. Right now is the test. We've grown up reading all of these scriptures our whole lives. Now it's test time. Who are you going to turn to? What god are you going to look to when the going gets tough?"

The Satanic forces could not have pressed their agenda this far unless the Almighty had extended their room for manoeuvre. Though they always sought to effect a genocide, they were kept in abeyance until the appointed time. Perhaps the timing of that time had something to do with our readiness to face it. I dare say none of us *feels* ready, but perhaps our life experiences thus far have prepared us. Then, if the Holy One has temporarily shifted the barriers in Satan's favour, then that same Lord of Hosts is Lord of Barriers and can mount them protectively around us.

Bear in mind, too, that the authorities are deathly afraid of us! And with far better reason.

Thrice is he armed that hath his quarrel just,
And he but naked, though locked up in steel,
Whose conscience with injustice is corrupted.

— SHAKESPEARE, *HENRY VI, PART II*

Their acts of censorship alone show how desperate they are to hide from the light, and how fearful. They are weak, they are cowards, cowering in the dark until the inevitable day when Justice finds them. No amount of riches or apparent security, nor all the sunshine of an island beach, could dispel the cold fear in their hearts, and nor will their torment end with their deaths.

Finally, on the subject of fear, I recall my favourite scene in Homer's *The Odyssey*, when Odysseus, the great warrior-strategist and hero of the Trojan War, is back at last in his Greek homeland of Ithaca. In Book 22, he and his son Telemachus, aided by Odysseus' swineherd and his cattle foreman, are pitted in a fight to the death against scores of men who, during his absence, had plundered his house, bedded his maids, and made a bid for his wife, Penelope.

When Odysseus runs out of arrows during the fight and sees that one of his enemies has managed to find some weapons, the "master of battle... felt his knees go slack,/ his heart sank." But, taking up spears, and with divine help, the four slay every remaining suitor.

Brothers and Sisters, the pulse may quicken, palms sweat, and knees tremble when the odds seem insurmountable but, like Odysseus who wins back his home, his Birthright, and his wife, we shall win back our Rights that await the hero's return to reclaim them.

PART VII

OUR BRUSH WITH FALSE AUTHORITY

The welfare of the people in particular has always been the alibi of tyrants... but in truth, the very ones who make use of such alibis know they are lies; they leave to their intellectuals on duty the chore of believing in them and of proving that religion, patriotism, and justice need for their survival the sacrifice of freedom.

— ALBERT CAMUS, SPEECH DELIVERED DEC. 7, 1955, AT A BANQUET IN HONOUR OF EDUARDO SANTOS, POLITICIAN AND EDITOR OF *EL TIEMPO*, WHO HAD BEEN DRIVEN OUT OF COLOMBIA BY THE DICTATORSHIP.

You may find the following alarming, but it gets better...

You wake up one morning to find the lights don't come on. Oh dear, a power cut. You'll have to boil water on the gas ring this morning. You go to the sink to fill a pot with water, but when you turn the tap on, only a trickle comes out, and then nothing. One flush of the toilet, and then no more. What the hell is going on?

You turn on your phone, there's some battery left. Find out what's happening. No phone signal. Alarmed, you look outside. Your neighbours are starting to gather on the street, trying in vain to get their dogs to stop barking, asking each other if they know anything, if anyone received a notice from the council. None did. At this point, a few are getting in their cars and driving off or walking hurriedly away with packed suitcases.

It is not long before a mechanical vibration fills the air. You look up. There are military helicopters overhead. The ground starts to shake. Armoured vehicles are driving along the street, accompanied by police cars with flashing lights. You and your neighbours rush back inside and lock the doors. But it is too late.

Your friends tried to warn you totalitarianism was coming, tried to warn you the government's COVID response was a ruse designed to kill and destroy, but you didn't listen. Those people were conspiracy theorists, covidiots, good for a laugh but not much else. No, you trusted the BBC, you sat glued to the television day after day to be bombarded with nightmarish scenarios about a new disease or a new variant. You heeded the messages to your mobile phone from the NHS telling you what to do with your body, you even clicked on those NHS messages pasted onto social media everywhere.

But there's no time to think about all that now. Masked men in black fatigues, armed with machine guns, are swarming over your street, going from house to house, rounding up anyone who can't or won't show their papers or QR code. The detained are taken to concentration camps to be enslaved, harvested for their pristine internal organs, forcibly injected, or otherwise disappeared. The circle has closed and, like thrashing fish scooped up in a net, the population is doomed.

Same are raped and kept as sex slaves. Some choose suicide over captivity or starvation. Meanwhile, the choicest land, houses, and vehicles now vacated are rewarded to the autocrats and their favourites, to complicit military and police personnel, and to compliant citizens, much as King William took the lands of the conquered English and parcelled them out among the Norman nobility in the 11th century.

Until that day, they had taken away your freedoms with your tacit consent, telling you it was for your own good and for the health of the nation. You dutifully wore your mask in shops and on public transport, shelled out for a barrage of meaningless tests, paid the exorbitant prices to stay in their shitty quarantine hotels, answered the summons to get shot, and let them compel your children to receive the life-altering toxin too. Was it all an elaborate con? Yes, but now it's too late to put the evil genie back in his bottle.

For you had conditioned the government to learn it

could get away with all this, that you were docile and willing to be pushed around, that it could strip your rights with impunity, that it could literally get away with murder. They did all this while lying to you, scaring you, and turning your island nation into a prison which you could only leave and enter with a special pass issued by the warden. But now, they don't need to pretend any more, the trap has sprung, and overnight you have been enslaved.

What am I doing here? Am I Fiver in *Watership Down* warning that the warren is about to be annihilated? Am I a Cassandra trying to tell fellow Brits that the vaccines are a Trojan horse? How long before an increasingly desperate British government pulls the trigger on such a totalitarian plan?

I have written this scenario not as a prophecy but as a warning if the government's sprint to totalitarianism is not checked—totalitarianism on a level and genocidal scale never seen before. I write it too as a call to mutiny in our armed forces, that if weaponry is to be used, to turn it on the autocrats and their operatives, not on the population you are supposed to serve and protect. And if there is prophecy in what I have described, may it be self-negating, not self-fulfilling. Nor, when I say 'you', do I mean the Reader of this book, but as a literary device to take you to the scene as one might watch a movie.

But understand this, that we are in the fight of our lives, a fight for the soul of Mankind, a fight which, like

Moses and the Israelites of old, **WE WILL WIN**. As I write this, a surge of joy affirms that yes, this is prophecy! The evil powers won't win this. Though they seem to be winning now, their downfall is written. Keep that in mind, follow it like the star that led the three kings to Jesus. That star is shining in the heavens, and they cannot pull it down, shift its position in the sky, or tell it to stop shining!

Here's what we do in the meantime...

ASSERTING AND UPHOLDING OUR RIGHTS

Disobedience is the true foundation of liberty. The obedient must be slaves.

— HENRY DAVID THOREAU,
CIVIL DISOBEDIENCE

So now for the rubber-meets-the-road moment where we suit action to word, and word to action. "Hold the line, stand your ground, uphold the rule of law, step into your sovereignty. The law is all there to protect you, but you're not going to get protected unless you know what it is and you uphold it," to repeat Anna de Buisseret's conclusion to her Parliament-Square interview.

By now, we're well versed in what the True Law is, but what do we do, say, or write when we face the agents and structures of legal lawlessness? Of course, there will be an element of improvisation in any situation, but I here endeavour to assemble best practices so we may be as thoroughly prepared and defended as possible.

And take our stand as *early* as possible! From bitter experience, I have learned it is always best to be sovereign at the outset of any encounter. It's so much more time-consuming, expensive, and exhausting to recover a situation afterwards. As the saying goes, "An ounce of prevention is better than a pound of cure."

Dolores Cahill is exemplary in this regard, especially when it comes to asserting Travel Rights. In her August 2021 interview with Clive de Carle, she explains how to deal with people "dressed up" as airport security, police, army, or judge if they are trying to obstruct her. It's worth listening to the whole interview, but here's a summary of the main actions she takes…

1. If dealing with several individuals, ask, "Which one of you is taking the responsibility for doing this?"

2. Ask that person, including any judge, if they are acting under their Oath. They have to answer yes. Tell them you accept their Oath.
Remember that the British Constable's Oath binds police to "upholding fundamental human rights" and "the law of the land" (not Admiralty code or corporate policy), so **once they answer yes, they can only uphold Common Law, and are not entitled to enforce acts and statutes.**

3. Find out their name.

4. Tell them the Rule of Law applies to you, which means you have the inalienable Rights of Freedom of Travel, Freedom of Speech, and bodily integrity.

5. Tell them any attempt to interfere with your freedom, or to infringe on your inalienable Right to Travel, is regarded under the Law as kidnapping or unlawful detention and carries a long prison sentence. "So if you're in the airport and they say they want to quarantine you, you say, 'No, I do not consent. Do not touch me. And then you tell them, 'I am free to go.' "

6. Inform them that if they touch you, it's assault, punishable by a prison term. "No-one can touch your body without your consent."

7. Inform them that if you are taken to prison, you will bring proceedings against them for unlawful detention and ensure they are personally and individually charged.

8. Understand, and tell them if necessary, that there is no indemnity or protection from individual liability in their role as police officer or judge.

Cahill has also interceded over the phone for detainees taken to a police station. It makes sense for each of us to prepare a hotline for ourselves, and the U.K. group Lawyers for Liberty (lawyersforliberty.uk) offers referral to 'freedom-friendly' law firms. I have also listed them in the Resources section (Appendix VIII) at the back of this book.

When it comes to international travel, imposition of tests, quarantines, and medical disclosures is deeply unlawful, and we are irrevocably empowered to refuse consent. "They know that what they're doing is criminal and unlawful," says Cahill, "infringing, forcing someone to have a PCR test when they don't consent, implying that it's mandatory quarantine at the airport when actually they are trying to entrap people and coerce them and deceive them into entering a contract which is not explicit and is misrepresented."

She continues, "What is being presented to us now, is that there is a health problem, but really that is masking a rule-of-law issue..." Anyone attempting to cause us harm, loss, or injury, whether a president or prime minister or someone dressed as police or judge or army, anyone who misrepresents the law or unlawfully detains another (kidnapping), has committed a criminal act, says Cahill. They are responsible in their private and personal capacity, and "can be sued and put in prison for the harm they do. There is no indemnity." Boris Johnson, she points out, is guilty of treason.

We can also learn from the stand taken by British life coach and fitness trainer, Harry Thomas, when landing in the U.K. from Brazil. Refusing to be quarantined, he was threatened with fines, unlawfully arrested by British police, and held for five hours in a cell. But, as he relates in a video testimony, by sticking to his inalienable Rights, he was released without quarantine or fine. "I am now a free man, no quarantine, no £2000 10-day hotel prison service, all charges dropped, and now I will be going after the individuals that harassed me and the officers that went against their oath."

He explains "how we are tricked and feared into decisions that we do not want to make" and too often give up our Rights when pressured into it, but "we must stick up for our truths and Rights and always keep our power." Here's the key takeaway from his testimony:

"BY LAW, THEY CAN NOT ENFORCE ANY RULES AND RESTRICTIONS ON TO US, UNLESS WE AGREE TO THEM."

Therefore, whenever any costumed one seeks to impose a rule, you can ask for Proof that you have consented to it which, of course, they can never supply.

INTERACTING WITH POLICE

It's helpful to know the standards expected of police officers according to the U.K. College of Policing's *Code of Ethics*. There, each officer pledges, "I will act with self-control and tolerance," "**Respect the rights of all individuals**," "Give and carry out lawful orders only," "Treat information with respect, and access or disclose it only in the proper course of my duties," and will not "abuse my position." Also, and this is especially important in the current environment, each officer promises to "Report, challenge or take action against the conduct of colleagues which has fallen below the standards of professional behaviour."

We also have *Magna Carta* to lean on, where "We will appoint as justices, constables, sheriffs, or bailiffs only such as know the law of the realm and mean to observe it well" (Article 45). Nor may any official "place a man on trial upon his own unsupported statement without producing credible witnesses to the truth of it" (Article 38).

Here's some more practical advice I gleaned from the documentary, *Strawman*...

1. Avoid entering into a verbal contract with the police, such as saying "yes" if they ask, "Do you understand?" What they really mean is, "Do you stand under me?" You do not! Use phrases like "I do not understand" and "I do not consent."

2. Avoid giving your name or date of birth. This means they can't do their paperwork. Ask, "Am I obliged to give you my details?" They have to answer no. If they say you do have to, they're lying and going against their Oath.

3. If helpful, read aloud the following, from Section 26 of the **Criminal Justice and Courts Act** (2015), where: any constable who "exercises the powers and privileges of a constable improperly," or to the detriment of another person, is liable on conviction to **imprisonment for up to 14 years and a fine.**

4. You don't have to engage in conversation with police. If they detain you without reasonable grounds, they're in breach of their Oath.

5. Ask, "Am I detained?" or "Am I free to go?"

6. If you are arrested, the custody officer at the police station must explain your Rights which

include: telling someone where you are, and getting free legal advice.

In one of his TikTok videos, Chris Edward advises those who live in Britain, America, Canada, Australia, New Zealand, or any other Common-Law jurisdiction:

> "If someone asks you a question, whether it's a policeman, someone in a court room or a council, you can simply say, 'I would like to remain silent.' If they continuously pressure you, say, 'Do I have the right to remain silent?' They will say, 'Yes, of course you do.'
>
> "And then remain silent. Do not say your name, and do not sign anything... If you do not speak your name, you are not entering yourself into their jurisdiction, and thus you are completely free... You do not have to answer questions. You do not have to sign anything."

Protests

The U.K.-based group, Liberty, have additional suggestions if you attend protests...

1. Leave your phone at home, and only bring an old phone with essential numbers on it. Make sure it is locked with a passcode and switch off any facial and fingerprint unlocking technology. You may wish to bring a portable phone charger if you have one.

2. Bring a notepad and pen to keep notes of any issues and to record the shoulder numbers of police officers.

3. Write important phone numbers on your arm. Include an emergency contact, a friend or family member, a solicitor with specialist knowledge about protests, and the Protest Support line operated by Green & Black Cross (07946 541 511), a project run by volunteers to help with legal matters arising from protest and actions.

4. Bring earplugs, a washcloth, and first-aid supplies.

5. Look out for Legal Observers wearing high-vis jackets. They are independent volunteers who monitor police, gather evidence of arrests, and counter any intimidation or unlawful behaviour protesters might face. They may be able to provide support. They will also have phone numbers of specialist solicitors.

Filming the police

If police become hostile, it is a good idea to film them. They're not allowed to prevent you. The U.K. Metropolitan Police's own website states, "Members of the public and the media do not need a permit to film or photograph in public places and police have no power to stop them filming or photographing incidents or police personnel."

This principle is even more firmly stated in a 2010 letter from Chief Constable Andrew Trotter, sent to all police stations, which reminds officers "citizen journalism is a feature of modern life..." and that...

> "There are no powers prohibiting the taking of photographs, film or digital images in a public place. Therefore members of the public and press should not be prevented from doing so... Once an image has been recorded, the police have no power to delete or confiscate it without a court order."

In the united States, the Right to film cops is founded on the **First Amendment**'s Freedom of the Press, that whatever our eyes can see in public, our camera can record.

Searches

If an officer intends to search you, they can only do so with objectively "reasonable suspicion" under the *Police and Criminal Evidence Act* (*PACE*) (1984), and must clearly state the reason and what they're looking for. The required set of procedures are encompassed by the mnemonic, GOWISELY...

- **G**rounds—a clear explanation of the reasons for the officer's search, i.e., why he finds you suspicious.
- **O**bject—what the officer will be looking for.

- Warrant—a warrant card to be produced if the officer is not in uniform.
- Identity—the officer must state their name and collar number.
- Station—the officer must identify the station at which they're based.
- Entitlement—the officer must inform you of your entitlement to a copy of the stop/search record.
- Legal—the officer must specify the legislation under which they're searching you.
- You—the Officer must clearly explain to you that you are being detained for the purpose of a search.

"If a police officer insists on searching you, do not resist," counsels the *Strawman* documentary. "Tell the officer you do not agree with the search and are being searched under duress." If the police do not follow the requirements of *PACE*, the search is unlawful, and an assault charge can be filed against the officer or officers.

If the officer is looking for drugs, then the *Drugs Act* (2005) determines, "**A drug offence search shall not be carried out unless the appropriate consent has been given in writing**" (Para. 3, subsection 3a).

INTERACTING WITH YOUR EMPLOYER

Monsters exist, but they are too few in number to be truly dangerous. More dangerous are the common men, the functionaries ready to believe and to act without asking questions.

— PRIMO LEVI

When governments are checked from imposing direct medical mandates, they can usually get servile employers to do their dirty work for them. By imposing treatment or testing as a condition of employment, these companies are effectively changing work contracts retrospectively and unilaterally. Then, like citizens of ancient Rome who had offended an emperor, the employee must choose either to take poison or to fall on the sword of financial ruin.

The **UDHR** states, "Everyone has the right to work"

(Article 23). This is expanded in the *ICESCR* where "In no case may a people be deprived of its own means of subsistence" (Part I, Article 1, Para. 2). Furthermore, the work must be freely chosen (Part III, Article 6, Para. 1) and come with "just and favourable conditions" (Part III, Article 7).

Employees are now being confronted with, to say the least, hostile work environments, and some, when already facing financial insecurity, are having to pay lawyers to uphold Justice against their oppressive taskmasters. There are some important steps you can take before it comes to that, though. The most obvious is to write a letter to your employer demanding respect for the contract of employment between you, which says nothing about vaccination or medical testing.

As Anna de Buisseret explains in another interview, "An employment contract is a contract between two people, equal parties to the contract. One party doesn't get to unilaterally impose a change in the contractual terms. You have to consent to it."

So a letter to your employer could say, "You cannot change my contract of employment without my agreement, and if you seek to do so, I will have Rights under constructive or unfair dismissal law."

You could also demand to know the medical status of all other employees, including all cases of AIDS, hepatitis, flu, measles, and mumps, and insist other employees are sectioned off if they have any illness that could spread, including the common cold. Conclude with "I would like to reach a satisfactory conclusion between us, but if that's not possible, I will have no choice but to raise this matter as an official grievance, and take legal action as may be necessary."

Another step de Buisseret recommends is to demand the employer give you an individual risk assessment under Regulation 3 of *The Management of Health and Safety at Work Regulations* (1999). This places a legal statutory duty on the employer to provide an individual risk assessment conducted by a qualified occupational-health physician. That assessment will include examination of the psychological harm of being in a coercive and hostile work environment.

The next stage would be to bring a grievance, and if the grievance is not upheld, to appeal it. "If the appeal is not upheld, don't resign. Consider the contract to be breached and bring a claim for constructive dismissal and breach of contract," de Buisseret advises.

In the specific case of healthcare practitioners seeking religious exemptions, refer to the letter in Appendix IV.

INTERACTING WITH YOUR CHILD'S SCHOOL

If there is anything more heinous than getting employers to coerce people to be injected, it is using schools to coerce children! If that is what you're facing, Lawyers for Liberty has prepared a template letter for parents at lawyersforliberty.uk/schooljabs. You can also opt to join the group's Whistleblowers' Register, meaning you have established a record of when you contacted the group about this matter.

MASKS

If you read Laura Dodsworth's book, *A State of Fear*, you will realize that masking requirements in shops or public transport were never about protecting health but were the imposition of behavioural scientists who "like masks because they convey a message of 'solidarity'... entirely unrelated to the scientific evidence regarding transmission."

But face masks are a medical intervention and require informed consent. "If a medical intervention (i.e., mask wearing or testing) is mandated," explain Lawyers for Liberty on their website, "or if an individual is coerced or manipulated into providing consent to that medical intervention, it would be in direct violation of the principle of Informed Consent and would be a breach of that person's legal rights."

Not wearing a mask is one small act of resistance we

can all practise, knowing Law is on our side. According to Lawyers for Liberty, "you don't need to produce evidence of your reason for not wearing a mask. You can simply say, 'I am exempt.' If the other party does not respect this, they are guilty of discrimination and can be sued in court."

This is not really a principled stand, though, is it? Exempt from what? Why ascribe to the state any authority to make an unlawful demand in the first place? The same fraudulent bargain is struck when individuals get fake vaccination certificates or test results to satisfy official demands.

As we have seen, the **UDBHR** states, "Any **preventive**, diagnostic and therapeutic medical intervention is only to be carried out with the **prior, free and informed consent** of the person concerned, based on adequate information." Masks are posing as a preventive intervention and, as such, require Informed Consent. Furthermore, we are not required to comply with an Act or statute to which we have not consented, nor any decree issued by politician or bureaucrat.

It is more powerful and truthful to say instead, "I am not required to." The medical aggressors will have no answer for that because there is none. If they ask you for evidence of this, you can point out that they have just attempted to breach your Medical Confidentiality. This stance applies equally if you encounter intrusive healthcare professionals. As we have seen, under the **NHS Code**, they're not allowed to share our medical information even among *themselves* without our written permission, much less with Government, police, border agents, or venues.

You can also ask them to show you the law that says you have to wear a mask. In the highly unlikely event they produce anything, ask them to show you where you signed it. Without your signature, it's not worth the air it's written on.

JUDICIAL REVIEW IN BRITAIN

Whenever a U.K. public authority has acted unlawfully or with bias or procedural unfairness, you can complete claim form 'N461' to mount a legal challenge in the form of a Judicial Review. You'll need to do so within three months of the decision, action, or inaction you want to challenge, or six weeks for planning decisions. Or, if the authority has acted contrary to the *HRA*, complete claim form 'N1' and file it at the relevant court building.

FINES

With regard to fines, the English *Bill of Rights* (1689) remains in statute, and says, "That all Grants and Promises of Fines and Forfeitures of particular persons before Conviction are illegall and void." This builds on *Magna Carta*...

> "No free man shall be seized or imprisoned, or stripped of his rights or possessions, or outlawed or exiled, or in any way destroyed, nor will we proceed with force against him, or send others to do so, except by the lawful judgment of his peers or by the law of the land [Common Law]" (Article 39).

In short, no-one may fine you or take any of your property without presenting evidence and obtaining a conviction in a court with trial-by-jury. Nor may they tax you, but that's another book.

My investigations suggest that the most effective strategy to adopt when false authorities or, more accurately, corporations disguised as authorities, make demands or impose levies, is to reply with 'conditional acceptance' or 'conditional offer', meaning we will agree to a demand only on condition that the enforcer or debt collector supply certain Proofs.

For example, as the demand is addressed to the ALL-CAPS legal fiction 'PERSON', I can ask for Proof of the implicit claim that I am that 'PERSON' and not a Living Man. I can ask for Proof of their claim that the levy was the result of a lawful investigation unmarred by prejudice. I can ask for clarification on the meaning of a word. I can ask for verification of the debt asserted and for an Invoice with a human signature on it. I can ask for Proof of the obligation to pay. I can ask for the lawful, two-party Contract that put us in a commercial relationship in the first place, and so on.

As they cannot supply these Proofs, I demolish their pretensions. If, after that, they persist with further collection efforts, then I can start levying financial penalties against them for each infringement. As @thequeenoffreedom explains in a TikTok video,...

"They cannot provide a contract, because there isn't one. I have done this with my credit card. I've done this with my council tax, my water, gas, and electric. And you will treat them all exactly the same. So you will ask each and every one of them, 'First of all provide the contract.' "

She continues, "Remember the only law: cause no harm, cause no loss. By not paying unlawful bills and fines, you are not causing anyone any loss. The only loss there would be to the company, which is a corporation, and a corporation cannot be a victim."

Although these corporations don't deserve our attention, respect, or even the time of day, it is deemed dishonour if we fail to respond at all when a contract is offered. We remain in honour by giving a response, and as we do not outright refuse the demand, the corporate courts have no controversy in which they can get involved.

"All men are born equal, and so nobody has the right to command you, made demands of you, or force you to do anything," writes David E. Robinson in the powerful little book, *Meet Your Strawman*. "The most that anyone can do is make you an offer to perform. Even though they may say that is is an 'Order', or a 'Demand', or a 'Summons', it is in reality an offer which you are free to accept or not as you so choose."

Generally speaking, we want to bring our contracts, transactions, and communications into the 'Private', and that includes creating or joining private member associations. That too, is another book.

PART VIII

OUR OVERTHROW OF FALSE AUTHORITY

The soul is a spark, but sparks do not shine in the bright light of day. As darkness deepens, the soul reveals its hidden light.

— DAVE MASON, *THE LAMP OF DARKNESS*

As we uphold our Rights, let us applaud those who have already struck a fierce constitutional blow on our behalf, such as Anna de Buisseret and the Lawyers for Liberty team, who are serving their 170-page Notice of Liability on skin-piercers.

"What we're doing is identifying people who are breaking the law," says de Buisseret, "and we're serving them with a Notice of Liability which says to the individual, 'You personally are causing harm. You are in breach personally of not only the Common Law but of international treaties, the European Conventions, U.K. domestic law.' "

And she knows by instinct what our Bible prophecies attest:

"Anyone who thinks they're not going to be blamed, they're not going to be held accountable, does not know their history. What happened after the last war, people's courts were formed in all jurisdictions. People knew who the perpetrators were, knew who the complicit people were, in their local communities. They found them, they took them from their homes, they put them in court, they judged them, and they handed down the sentence."

THE NEW NAZI HUNTERS

The Spirit's wind will sweep the land,
Its reach from shore to shore,
The Earth will shake with thunderous sound,
Then hear my lions roar.

Turn upward your eyes to gaze upon
Heaven's open door.
I come for you, my ready bride,
And parted never more.

Look up, look up, my faithful ones.
Nigh is your reward.

— RAPTURE RESCUE, YOUTUBE VIDEO,
APR. 21, 2021

When Justice returns, prosecutors will invoke several articles of international Rights declarations, including the *Nuremberg Code*. The *Rome Statute* of the ICC will also play a prominent role. We have already looked at *Rome* Article 7, which lists Crimes against Humanity. These include **"persecution against any identifiable group,"** apartheid, and "Imprisonment or other severe deprivation of physical liberty."

Rome Article 6, applying to Genocide, will also come into play. In addition to killing members of a group, the definition includes serious bodily or **mental harm**, inflicting **"conditions of life calculated to bring about its physical destruction,"** and "measures intended to prevent births."

Rome Article 8, on War Crimes, should also keep prosecutors busy. Here, the definition includes biological experiments, subjecting persons "to physical mutilation or to medical or scientific experiments of any kind," and using poisonous "liquids, materials or devices."

Are we clear? Anna de Buisseret is fiercely joined in this cause by fellow Rights campaigner and former nurse, Kate Shemirani, who has put the autocrats on notice. "You are going to stand trial while there's breath in my body," she said in an August 2021 interview with Charlie Ward, "and I pray that I live long enough to see it because I myself personally, for every child in this country, and every vulnerable child and adult, I will be the new Nazi hunter. I'm not going to stop."

Of course, the mainstream media have done their best to smear Shemirani. Wikipedia describes her as "a British conspiracy theorist, anti-vaxxer, and former nurse who lost her licence to practise in 2020 for misconduct. She is best known for promoting conspiracy theories about COVID-19, vaccinations and 5G technology."

Well, they would say that, wouldn't they? They've said similar about de Buisseret, Dolores Cahill, and many more outspoken heroes of this age. Haven't the censors run out of fingers to plug the dike by now?

Courageous forces are aligning to prosecute the criminal pharma cabal. In December 2021, the International Criminal Court accepted a Crimes-Against-Humanity filing (Reference OTP-CR-473/21) against Boris Johnson and his coterie, along with Bill Gates, Anthony Fauci, pharmaceutical executives, and others in the medical-industrial complex, for violations of *Nuremberg* and of Articles 6, 7, and 8 of *Rome*.

Later that month, Dr Sam White, solicitors Lois Bayliss and Philip Hyland, and retired police constable Mark Sexton filed a criminal complaint at Hammersmith Police Station, London (Crime Number 6029679/21) citing...

misfeasance in public office, misconduct in public office, conspiracy to commit grievous bodily harm, conspiracy to administer a poisonous and noxious substance to cause serious harm and death, gross negligence, manslaughter, corporate manslaughter, corruption, fraud, blackmail, murder, conspiracy to commit murder, terrorism, genocide, torture, crimes against humanity, false imprisonment, multiple breaches of our human rights, war crimes, multiple breaches of the *Nuremberg Code* (1947), and multiple breaches of the *Human Rights Act* (1998).

A treason charge is also likely to follow. The Criminal Complaint reads...

"In accordance with Section 3 of the Criminal Law Act (1967), we now call on you to assist us in the closure of all vaccine centres within your jurisdiction. The Criminal Law Act (1967) Section 3 states, '**A person may use such force as is reasonable in the circumstances in the prevention of crime**, or in effecting or assisting in the lawful arrest of offenders or suspected offenders or of persons unlawfully at large.' These gene therapy drugs are the murder weapon. This is the weapon that the U.K. government is using to hurt, maim, and kill millions of people in the U.K.

"The evidence must be seized by the police as part of this investigation. It is incumbent on you to do that without fail in all police jurisdictions around the U.K. The Criminal Law Act (1967) gives any man or woman the authority and the power to prevent crime. We also have authority to use force as is reasonable, necessary, and proportionate in order to prevent that crime from happening.

"You may be resistant to this. However, there is now a live criminal investigation in place. You have a duty to protect the people. You are public servants who we pay with public taxes and public money. You work for us. If crime, injury, serious harm, and death is being committed, it is incumbent on your office of Constable on Oath which you swore to protect us the people from said harm.

"If you are in attendance, it is your duty to gather evidence and seize the weapon which, in this case, are the vaccine vials. These vaccine vials should then be taken into protective custody and detained in your property evidence stores to be independently forensically tested as a matter of urgency.

"This is a fact in law. The law is the same, whether you are a police constable in uniform or whether you are a citizen, a man or woman that is sovereign. The police have a duty. That duty is to respond and act accordingly. If the police fail to do their job, they are committing an offence of misconduct in public office and perverting the course of justice. If they know offenders are responsible for these crimes and they do anything to assist those offenders or prevent those crimes from being detected, or deliberately frustrate the criminal investigation, they are also guilty of an offence of assisting a known offender.

"May I remind you that you work for the people, you do not work for the government. It is the government ministers, the civil servants, and the media bosses who are committing these disgusting and heinous atrocities against millions of people throughout the United Kingdom.

"It is ridiculous to expect us to address members of Parliament. They are the very people committing these crimes. We do not speak to the offenders. That is the job of the police, and these people must be arrested. So we now demand that you assist us in forcing all vaccine centres within your jurisdiction to cease and desist with immediate effect."

Following this declaration, plaintiff Mark Sexton clarifies in a January 2022 video that we are all entitled under the *Criminal Law Act*, Section 3, to intervene against crime ourselves. He also invokes *PACE* (the aforementioned *Police and Criminal Evidence Act* of 1984), Section 24A, by which a person other than a constable may arrest without a warrant anyone who is in the act of committing, or has committed, an indictable offence, including injury to any other person, if "it is not reasonably practicable for a constable to make it instead."

Thus, when it comes to injection centres, we are required first to remind any police present that it is their duty to shut the centre down and to seize vials for evidence. If they do not act, then we are empowered under Section 24A of *PACE* to shut them down ourselves and to carry out arrests. "The police know this," Sexton adds. "They use Section 24. Their laws are our laws. Their powers are our powers. But we employ them to carry out these laws and powers with consent."

CONCLUSION

We will not be driven by fear into an age of unreason, if we dig deep in our history and our doctrine, and remember that we are not descended from fearful men – not from men who feared to write, to speak, to associate, and to defend causes that were, for the moment, unpopular.

— EDWARD R. MURROW, 1954

As Shakespeare said of Love, "It is the star to every wandering bark." So are Rights declarations to us, enduring stars of guidance untouched by the storms playing out beneath. Listen, for example, to these opening words of the **UDHR**...

"The Universal Declaration promises to all the economic, social, political, cultural and civic rights that underpin a life free from want and fear. They are not a reward for good behaviour. They are not country-specific, or particular to a certain era or social group. They are the inalienable entitlements of all people, at all times, and in all places."

Words this majestic must have been written in love, and God is love. This charter, and others like it, give us the words to rebuke the propaganda and lies if we will but assert them. Their power overthrows the diktats of men, proud men, dressed in their little brief authority, most ignorant of what they're most assured.[1]

Bravely we set forth, and whenever our vessel nears a shore, we look with the eyes of discernment to know whether it offers true sanctuary or sings a siren song promising security at the cost of our souls.

Now, you may say our charters and constitutions are mere collections of words, and what good are words against such murderous hatred now unleashed upon the world? I answer, what are the orders of politicians but words? And what are Acts of Parliament or Congress but words? And when words are empty, as Homer reminds us in his epic about a sea voyage, they are evil.[2]

We are in a fight to the death, whether we like it or not, and our enemy is like a prowling lion, ever hunting for someone to devour (*1 Peter* 5:8). His malice shocks us. We gasp at his brazen lies, shudder at his cowardly tactics, and seethe as he tortures, maims, and kills for pleasure, but we have authority to overcome *all* of his power (*Luke* 10:19).

We wanted to be left in peace to enjoy our lives and

pursue our happiness, but now that we see Hatred pursuing our destruction, we are stirred with the spirit of battle. As Shakespeare's King Henry V says on the eve of Agincourt (IV.i),...

We would not seek a battle as we are,
Nor, as we are, we say we will not shun it.

Henry then isolates himself to pray...

O God of battles, steel my soldiers' hearts.
Possess them not with fear. Take from them now
The sense of reckoning, lest the opposed numbers
Pluck their hearts from them.

The next day, he and his army, though tired and depleted, achieve a stunning victory over "The confident and overlusty French."

Do not overestimate our foe now. At heart, he is weak and deathly afraid, while his craven agents know not what they do or what they say or what they think and, in their haste for satisfaction, are making fatal errors along the way. Their very logic is rooted in fear, the truth is not in them, and their protestations of care and service are but clanging cymbals that can never drown out the divine whisper in our hearts. Their ultimate end, I say again, echoes that of Pharaoh and his cohorts drowned in the Red Sea. In the words of author and broadcaster, Mike Adams, "The demonic anti-human forces that currently control Big Tech, Big Media, Big Pharma, and Big

202 A. LE ROY

Government, they will be dismantled and defeated and ultimately destroyed by God."[3]

Until then, I marvel at the resolve, courage, dedication, and resourcefulness of allies who have emerged in these dark times, image bearers of the divine, brothers and sisters afire with the Spirit that overturns tables in our temples defiled. Most defiled of all in these times is the body itself, the last frontier of resource extraction, a goldmine to be drilled and plundered by corporate opportunists until, used up and depleted, it is discarded as medical waste. Yes, into this holy place they have brought many abominations that cause desolation, to echo *Matthew* 24:15.

This is also the time to be wise as serpents (*Matthew* 10:16), to probe the air as a snake would, and to sniff out deception. It is a time to know and hear the Shepherd's voice (*John* 10:16) and to heed only his true prophets (*Matthew* 7:15). I dare say that, as a seeker of truth, you have already cultivated this skill, but a handy rule of thumb is to follow the money. Who is paying the latest false prophet? Who has sponsored his statements? And do his words, or the consequence of those words, accord with or defile international Rights protections?

You have witnessed others compliantly follow into annihilation, even as they bleated a chorus of disapproval to denounce you. But you have joined a new alliance of black sheep.

Above all, it is time to step into our power. In my braver moments, I consider it a gift that we now have such obvious villains, and such demonstrable villainy, to oppose. They call forth our greatness, so that the glory of God may be revealed in us.

Here, I quote Dr Zelenko again: "I see the transformation of humanity as a whole into a much more enlightened state of consciousness where truth and goodness will reign, and ultimately the revelation of the divine."

If, on the other hand, you are part of the state's apparatus for enforcing unconstitutional orders and atrocity, beware how you treat protestors, naysayers, whistleblowers, doctors of conscience, investigative journalists, and civic-minded citizens, for whatsoever you do to them, you do to Christ (*Matthew* 25:41-46), and he will embrace you or discard you accordingly.

I'm not just talking to physical enforcers such as police, but to hospitals and medical professionals, and to financial institutions now called on to persecute dissenters. Welcome a prophet as a prophet, and receive a prophet's reward (*Matthew* 10:41), but incur a prophet's curse, and you shall find it carries a power that neither you nor your weapons nor your wealth, nor all your political or mercenary connections, can even begin to imagine, much less oppose.

Remember too, that there never was, nor ever will be, any comfort or validity in the defence, "I was just following orders." It didn't work in **Nuremberg** 1.0; it won't work in **Nuremberg** 2.0.

If you do not, then this decree is for you: You will not eat, though your plate is full; you will not sleep, though your bed is soft; you will go to your torment, despised of

God and Mankind; you will go to your doom. This is decreed in Heaven, and now effected on Earth. Amen, and so be it.

Love compels us to act and speak now lest, "as we remain silent, the destruction continues," to quote the British doctor Lucie Wilk again. And in our speaking, let us waste no words trying to persuade others that government oppression is wrong on the shaky ground that current conditions do not warrant it. Missing the point, missing the point, so dangerously and utterly missing the point! No conditions could *ever* warrant it. No emergency, not even another Black Death, could warrant it. Ever! Rights are eternal, the rulings of politicians pissing in the wind, and our constitutional cause transcends all other contested discourse. If they call you an idiot for exercising your sovereignty and declining their medicine, so what? International Law protects our Right to be an idiot!

And no, we are NOT looking to 'balance' individual Rights against some tyrannical depiction of the collective good. No, our Rights are our North, our South, our East, our West, our working week and our Sunday rest, to paraphrase Auden. We are not going to compromise them or bargain them away. Life is simply not worth living without them. What is the point of deferring death at all costs only to preserve a life so joyless and locked down that it is not worth living? I say again, and for the third time in this book, we are **CONSTITUTIONAL EXTREMISTS**!

Nor is there any point in arguing with the tyrants

themselves, trying to persuade them to be a little less unkind to us. Nor, when they feel cornered and start talking about concessions, shall we pay them any more heed than Odysseus paid Penelope's suitors who wanted to negotiate just before he slaughtered them.

Seared of conscience, the puppet tyrants don't care in the least what is reasonable, fair, or just, and will remain determined, for as long as they think they can get away with it, to impose top-down destruction on the lives they have sworn to protect. There is but one recourse left to us now...

MASS COORDINATED SABOTAGE OF THE AGENDA; DESTRUCTION OF VACCINE AND SURVEILLANCE INFRASTRUCTURE; DISOBEDIENCE TO MEDICAL MANDATES AND DECREES; ARREST AND PROSECUTION OF ALL IN THE 'VACCINE' SUPPLY CHAIN, INCLUDING MEDIA PROPAGANDISTS.

(AND arrest of all in the 5G supply chain too, though that's another book.) As Kate Shemirani reminds us, "We can only be abused if we allow ourselves to be." What if thousands of us descended on the new internment camps and reduced them to rubble? What if we tore down the shelves of vile vials? What if everyone told to show their medical status refused, knowing that the very demand was an abomination? What a mighty impulse of joy would the world receive!

Medical confidentiality is at the core of everything

we've looked at. If all upheld this one principle, then none of the horrors predicated upon its breach could follow. I mean, how can people hate others who made a different medical choice, as mainstream media so eagerly call on them to do, if they don't know whom to hate?

Again, I appeal for unity between 'vaxxed' and 'unvaxxed'. We have a common enemy who regards all of us as disposable—as tadpoles, to return to my *Parable of the Frogs*. The sooner we all realize this, the quicker sanity returns.

To help with that, here's a thought experiment for any reader who has been injected. Imagine that the false powers declare one day that oops, turns out that *you* are in the group showing higher levels of infection and transmission. *You* are now among the outcasts, barred from society, and denied hospital treatment, so that the newly exalted 'purebloods' can take your place. Or worse, imagine *you* are in the group to be exterminated in concentration camps.

You would regard this as a totalitarian violation of your Rights, wouldn't you? Then, under the **Royal Law** of loving others as yourself, why would you think it OK to do this to today's nominated group of outcasts?

The so-called leaders don't love you, never have, never will. You may be a favoured child of the patriarchs today, a convenient tool to be used against those who resist, but tomorrow, when you have served your purpose, off you go to the hells you assigned to others. Would you not rather stand up for the Rights of all now so that your future, and that of your children, can be safeguarded too?

I also call for unity between police or army personnel of conscience and civilians. The choice for appointed enforcers is stark: fealty to life, to your public oath, and to eternal values; or obedience to orders and secret oaths, to a living death, and everlasting torment. Which is it?

Every warrior's boot used in battle
and every garment rolled in blood
will be destined for burning,
will be fuel for the fire.

— *ISAIAH* 9:5

As I just said to cheerleaders of Government, do you think your political and corporate masters care one jot about you? What will they do to you and your children and your loved ones, once you have outlived your usefulness? Send you off with a nice pension so that you can say of yourself, as Aleksandr Solzhenitsyn would say of you, "I am cattle, I am a coward. I seek only warmth and to eat my fill."?[4] Is it a company house you're after, or a company car? Don't kid yourself. You too were a useful tadpole for a while, ready to oppress and kill other tadpoles, but the frogs will never allow you to become one of them, or to share in their bounty.

As Sarah (of the family) Feeley says in the *Strawman* documentary,...

"People need to get educated. People need to start waking up and realize what's going on around them.

Generally, people only tend to give a damn what's happening when it's actually on their doorstep and it's happening to them. But we can't wait for that to happen, we need to realize that we're all one and the same. We all need to look out for each other and protect each other because we've got a system now that's been built up around us, we've got a corporate web of an empire that's completely taken over every aspect of our lives."

In his essay, *The Power of the Powerless*, Czech dissident and playwright turned statesman Václav Havel documents the kind of transformational change that comes about when we realize "not standing up for the freedom of others... meant surrendering one's own freedom." He chronicles how a young Czech rock band, The Plastic People of the Universe, by refusing to obey the totalitarian state in Czechoslovakia, sparked a movement in 1989 that brought the system down.

"For the crust presented by the life of lies is made of strange stuff. As long as it seals off hermetically the entire society, it appears to be made of stone. But the moment someone breaks through in one place, when one person cries out, 'The emperor is naked!', when a single person breaks the rules of the game, thus exposing it as a game, everything suddenly appears in another light and the whole crust seems then to be made of a tissue on the point of tearing and disintegrating uncontrollably."

A cursory glance at history shows, alas, a litany of atrocity, but there was never a time when the totalitarian assault was this, well, total in its geographic range, nor the options for flight so few. Even Florida, to which many have fled, is servant to medical tyranny. In May 2021, Governor Ron DeSantis signed state legislation, SB 2006, confirming the state's health officer may, "upon declaration of a public health emergency," order an individual...

> "to be examined, tested, vaccinated, treated, isolated, or quarantined for communicable diseases... If there is no practical method to isolate or quarantine the individual, the State Health Officer may use any means necessary to vaccinate or treat the individual. Any order of the State Health Officer given to effectuate this paragraph is immediately enforceable by a law enforcement officer."

> — TITLE XXIX, CHAPTER 381,
> SECTION 00315

I dare say that, should Republicans retake the Oval Office and Congress, the boot of tyranny will merely shift to the other foot. Then it will be a politically motivated Democratic Party, rather than a constitutionally principled one, denouncing medical mandates, while those who had initially fled California's COVID tyranny will flood back in, looking for sanctuary.

I agree with Anna de Buisseret's assessment that we're seeing "the biggest crimes against humanity ever committed in the history of humankind." But I am also encouraged by her message that time is on our side, that the powers-that-shouldn't-be are not only on the wrong side of the Law but on the wrong side of history, and that "We are going to get the right results."

Time will also recruit allies to the constitutional cause as more people realize governments have not only betrayed their Social Contract with us but are waging undeclared war against us. As podcast host Bret Weinstein observes, "This is a failure that has breached the walls of medicine and is now toppling the most basic elements of our societal agreement with each other."

Yet, having outdone themselves this time, the autocrats have done themselves in! They have pushed the agenda too far, got too greedy, tipped their hand, given the game away, and like the jubilant murderers who nailed Christ to the Cross and thought to get away with it, have exposed themselves to Justice resurrected. And what a glorious and healing resurrection it will be when a new kingdom is established on Earth and when, to the increase of the Holy One's merciful reign, there will be no end (*Isaiah* 9:7).

Are we in the end times of *Revelation*? Or is this a rehearsal for the end-times, as the tyrants maim and indoctrinate the next generation of psychopaths to be even worse than the last? Either way, the field of battle lies ahead. What a glorious time to be alive!

CODA

On the very day this book was to be published, I had a dream that revealed more about the power structures we are contending with. It warrants this last-minute inclusion...

I am helping to bring a patient into a hospital, but when I go in, the building is something like a church, yet it feels menacing. I go up a winding staircase and along a narrow corridor. I sense danger, and fear I will be trapped in there. I drop the patient off. I want to protect her, but fear what will happen to me if I stay. I go back down the winding staircase and make my way out quietly. As I leave the building by a side door, an old man in charge of the building exits by the main door. He shouts, "Fire her!" at a woman on his staff.

   I make my way along a street. Now, I am in some kind of wheelchair and, moving slowly by the strength of my hands, I fear being caught because I can't get away from the building fast

enough. But I have two brothers walking beside me on each side.
The one on my left turns and smiles at me. His face is all love
and benevolence. Though I can only move slowly, he will
protect me.

Upon waking, I recall a commentary by Russell Brand about World Economic Forum (WEF) co-founder, Klaus Schwab, and Schwab's demand a woman on his staff be fired for using his parking spot while he'd been away. So I realize that Schwab, hitherto unmentioned in this book, is presiding over today's unholy alliance of hospital with Satanic temple. His centrality to the plot is only confirmed by a BBC 'Reality Check' analysis that attempts to dismiss 'conspiracy theories' about his 'Great Reset' agenda.

With its Forum of Young Global Leaders—begun in 1992 as Global Leaders of Tomorrow—the WEF has groomed today's crop of tyrant notables, including Justin Trudeau of Canada, Emmanuel Macron of France, Jacinda Ardern of New Zealand, and European Commission president, Ursula von der Leyen. Schwab himself boasted,

"When I mention our names like Mrs. Merkel, even Vladimir Putin and so on, they all have been Young Global Leaders of the World Economic Forum. But what we are very proud of now is the young generation like Prime Minister Trudeau, the president of Argentina, and so on, that we penetrate the cabinets. So yesterday I was at the reception for Prime Minister Trudeau, and I know that half of this cabinet, or even more [than] half of this cabinet, are actually Young Global Leaders of the World Economic Forum. It's true in Argentina, and it's true in France now."

I gather that Schwab expects a Nobel Peace Prize for his services to Humanity. Well, if they can give it to the likes of Barack Obama, Aung San Suu Kyi, and Abiy Ahmed, he might just get one. His agenda, though, is anything but peaceful. Schwab's lizard sidekick at the WEF, author Yuval Noah Harari, said in an interview:

> "People could look back in a hundred years and identify the coronavirus epidemic as the moment when a new regime of surveillance took over, especially surveillance under the skin which, I think, is maybe the most important development of the twenty-first century, this ability to hack human beings, to go under the skin, collect biometric data, analyze it, and understand people better than they understand themselves."

At the WEF annual Davos forum in 2020, Harari advised, "We humans should get used to the idea that we are no longer mysterious souls. We are now hackable animals."

That Harari could be so open about this dystopian agenda shows the WEF is operating in a bubble of delusion, completely untethered from reality. It seeks to desecrate the Creator's image in us, and assumes we will welcome our own enslavement under the most intrusive surveillance imaginable.

One shorthand word for all this is 'transhumanism', which expects to upgrade human beings by technology. It includes, in Schwab's own words to the Chicago Council on Global Affairs in 2019, "a fusion of our physical, digital, and biological identities."

It's a hideous idea and, in these early days of the attempt, clumsy and botched, resulting in all manner of mutilation. But that's not a problem for the 'globalists', who regard us as guineapigs. As New Zealand doctor Sam Bailey observes in a February 2022 commentary,

> "The globalists have some sick agendas they are attempting to roll out, and they want to disconnect us from spirituality in their perverted plan for humanity. Dr Harari and his Davos buddies are so unconscious that they think they are gods. To them, you are livestock that is ripe for their transhumanist experiments and eventual enslavement."

I ask myself why old men like Schwab and Fauci and Gates would be so intent on clearing the planet of us 'useless eaters' when they have so little time left to enjoy it, and must then face hellish consequences in the hereafter. There can be only one reason...

THESE MORONS ACTUALLY BELIEVE THEY HAVE FOUND SOME KEY TO IMMORTALITY THROUGH THE SACRIFICE OF OTHERS.

Here's the thing about false prophets. What comes

out of their mouth is, by definition, false prophecy, meaning that which shall NOT come to pass. When the plans of our gracious and compassionate God are to prosper us and not to harm us, to give us hope and a future, do you think an arrogant pipsqueak like Harari, with his plans for a 'digital dictatorship', could succeed? The idea is laughable!

Yet I shudder to think what ritualistic horrors are now being practised in secret temples, given that wealthy individuals routinely harvest the blood of young people in a bid to extend their own lives. In a December 2019 *MintPress* article on the booming blood market, Alan Macleod reported, "Teenager blood is in high demand in, of all places, Silicon Valley, where anti-aging technologies are the latest trend. One company, Ambrosia, charges $8,000 per treatment to aging tech executives, infusing them with the blood of the young." Among the keenest customers, according to Macleod, is PayPal co-founder Peter Thiel who, in his own words, stands against "the ideology of the inevitability of the death of every individual."

We cannot expect any check of conscience from this cult. The WEF claims, in a January 2022 article citing unnamed 'experts', that vaccine mandates are not Human-Rights violations: "Not really, say experts on actual human rights violations," the article asserts. "In fact, some point to the more fundamental right of everyone to be protected from COVID-19—particularly as variants continue to disproportionately impact the unvaccinated."

This purported Right to be protected from an ephemeral disease is an invention that our ancestors never thought to insert into their own constitutions, much less nominate as "more fundamental" than all the other Rights, based on lasting values, that have stood the test of time. As we saw near the start of this book, there is no Law more fundamental than the 'Royal Law', the Law written by the Author of Life himself, to love others as we love ourselves. That means no-one gets to impose their medical will on someone else. This should be self-evident, but we are living in an age when we must once again tear down Satanic arguments and pretensions that set themselves up against the knowledge of God (2 *Corinthians* 10:5).

And what about the word, 'mandate'? Is it any coincidence that 'mandate' is the very word Freemasons use when the head of a lodge issues instructions to members of the lodge? Was it a lodge that I saw in my dream? If governments are going for medical enforcement, why not use more commonplace terms such as 'order', 'command', 'requirement', 'regulation', or 'policy'? And why say 'mandatory' if 'required' or 'compulsory' is meant?

Secret-society coordination, I have come to realize, is the key explanation for the globally orchestrated tyranny we have seen since the COVID era. The reason doctors can routinely desecrate the *Hippocratic Oath* is because they have sworn a secret oath that usurps it and because they have participated in horrific initiation rites that have seared their consciences into silence. They wear white coats by day but black robes by night, kill with knives in the darkness but with needles in the light, and they have turned hospital beds into sacrificial altars.

Secret oaths are also the reason that politicians can flout their oaths to constitution, bureaucrats their oaths of office, and police their **Constable's Oath**. Above ground, they are organized in corporate pyramid structures, but below ground in the hidden depths, they are mirrored by an inverted pyramid whose apex descends to Satan himself. Freemasons think to rise when they progress through their 33 levels, but in reality, they are descending with each promotion deeper and deeper into the abyss.

Or think of the governments, agencies, corporations, hospitals, and institutions as a poison tree producing poison fruit. As a tree's visible structure is mirrored by its root structure underground, the root system of today's tyranny is bound with secret oaths, secret rituals, and secret pacts, and nourished with the blood of innocents. Our visible societies have become infested at every level with secret-society parasites doing the bidding of Lucifer, who is Satan masquerading as an angel of light, and of his infernal conspirators, Baal and Moloch.

Yet they shall find no chamber, dungeon, or tunnel deep enough or dark enough to hide them and their crimes from the searing light of the Holy One, whose penetrating gaze I now direct from Heaven upon them. From Heaven, we unmask and expose them, that they are unmasked and exposed on Earth, so that all shall know who they are, and what they are, and what they have done, and whom they serve.

These days, Christians waste a lot of time debating where we are in the End-Times calendar, looking for a Rapture any day now to lift us beyond the tyrant's reach. They argue too about whether this divine rescue operation occurs before or during the 'Tribulation'. I prefer to keep things simple, to know that Christ has given me authority to overcome all the power of the enemy, that he who is in me is greater than he who is in the tyrant parasites, and that when I resist the devil, he will flee from me. So it is written, and so shall it be.

Much love,
Abdiel LeRoy

INTRODUCTION TO
KNOW YOUR LAWFUL RIGHTS
BOOK 2 IN 'BATTLE MANUALS FOR FREEDOM'

The elite's goal is disturbingly straightforward: to hollow out the individual, leaving an empty shell while stripping away the soul.

— A LILY BIT, *THE EXPOSE,* MAR. 15, 2024

We were born into slavery, but until recently, most of us did not know it. With subtle treachery, banks, corporations, and governments have stolen our Birthright. Spiritual vampires, they have drained us of our time and energies, even of life itself, to enrich themselves. It took the atrocities of COVID to alert us to this, to shake us awake, and to break the spell that has been perpetrated against Mankind for centuries and even millennia.

Some were aware of the tyrants' genocidal plans even

before COVID, and for that you have my deepest respect. You did your best to warn everyone what evil was afoot, and you saved lives. Though you were censored and reviled, you stuck to your message, and then I joined you to expose how broad and deep is the conspiracy against us. In early 2022, I published *The COVID Protocols: Upholding Your Rights in Authoritarian Times,* now retitled *Know Your Medical Rights.* I thought this would be enough, but when the despotism spread from the medical arena to every other area of life, I realized COVID was just the first round in a barrage of assaults aimed at demolishing our lives, our livelihoods, and all that makes life worth living. I would need to write more books.

I agree with Dr. Rima Laibow's observation, in a March 2024 interview with Maria Zeee, that...

"There is no aspect of human life which will be allowed to continue as we know it, as we value it. And most of all, what is being destroyed is the capacity to love and to trust one another. So we are being separated from our wisdom, from our bodies, from our DNA, from our children, from our property, from our very capacity to bring food forth from the Earth. We are being separated from our ability to think, to communicate, all of it in the interest of a vast and total suppression of humanity into a slave caste that can never rise up again. To which my response is, 'No! Out! I want out of your system!' "

Yes, Dr. Rima has poetically described the breadth of tyranny now afoot, but I am astonished too by its depth.

It starts with international puppet masters, usually described as 'globalists', who take their orders from secret societies and the infernal influences that inspire them. Then, the tyranny is channeled through their network of despots installed in national governments and other corporations.

The infestation doesn't stop there, though, for regional and local governments, county councils, town councils, planning departments, and even school boards and housing associations are fully on board with the despotic agenda of enslavement and destruction, either as complicit operatives or as useful idiots.

Police forces, meanwhile, corporate henchmen and bandits for hire, are enforcing all of this. How refreshing it would be if just one stood up and said, "No sir. That's an unlawful order." What a revelation if just one upheld their Oath. Instead, we are treated to the shameful spectacle of police beating up, trampling, and irradiating protesters, menacing journalists, arresting people for praying in public, and even issuing tickets against those who feed the homeless. And that's just what they do in public. Meanwhile, they give protective escort to today's agents of doom when angry crowds come too close.

COVID also taught me a new word: democide, defined in the *Collins Dictionary* as "the killing of members of a country's civilian population as a result of its government's policy, including by direct action, indifference, and neglect." I now realize that governments of the West have been doing this for decades, but they got much more unsubtle and extreme about it with COVID, both with the murderous protocols deployed in hospitals and nursing homes, then with the coerced poison injections they called 'vaccines'. Since then, among many vectors of attack, they have gone after our food, our fuel, and funds too.

I laugh when I hear people talk about "government overreach" or when they say, "The government doesn't have your best interests at heart." OK, I suppose you could call genocide 'overreach', but strip away the varnish and you will see a regime that wants to enslave you, to extract every ounce of value it can from your life and labour then, when you've nothing left to give, to discard you as cheaply as possible and add your corpse to the growing pile of medical waste. And if that's too much of a mouthful, your government simply wants to kill you!

Nor are legislators doing much to check rogue administrations. As 'Health Ranger' Mike Adams said in a May 2024 broadcast,...

"All they do every single day in the halls of Congress is they figure out, 'How can we hurt America today? How do we harm the American people? How do we vote against the interests of the American people?' They're straight-up traitors. Every single day, they conspire of how to destroy this country from within."

And that conspiracy is entirely 'legal' in the sense that politicians, or rather their handlers, have drawn up documents that not only codify their thefts and murders but shield them from consequence with so-called 'legal immunity'. I tend to agree with Max Igan's encapsulation, in a February 2024 broadcast, that "Every single problem on Earth exists because it has been legislated to exist."

Which brings me to a central theme of this book, and that is to draw a clear distinction between 'legal' and 'lawful', for they are very different things and usually contrary. 'Legal' pertains to the legislation that men create—Acts, statutes, rules, regulations, decrees, and codes, the injustice of which corporate courts cement with their rulings. 'Lawful', by contrast, belongs only to the Creator, whom to serve is Freedom (*John* 8:36; *2 Corinthians* 3:17) and whose burden is light (*Matthew* 11:28-30), and it respects our inherent Rights and dignity. These Rights may be enshrined in constitutions but they don't depend on constitutions for their existence or applicability.

As Living Men and Women operating in the Lawful, which is our Birthright, we are wholly above the Legal. Indeed, as three-dimensional beings, we are an entire *dimension* above the Legal, which operates only in the two-dimensional realm of words on paper. Those words cannot reach up from the page, grab us by the neck, and pull us down into their flattened space, though that is what their devisers intend. No, those documents are dead to us, and we refuse to breathe life into them by consenting to them with our signatures. In the three-dimensional realm where we live and move and breathe and have our beings, Government cannot even touch us, much less dictate to us.

Yet politicians, along with enforcers and

commentators, routinely ascribe to tyrant code the false label of 'Law'. It's all fiction, all counterfeit. By True Law, or 'Common Law', those who deliberately do harm must face Justice, while the falsely accused are innocent if there is no victim.

More troubling still, the fallacy of calling rules made up by men and women 'Law' is echoed by so-called alternative voices, Freedom warriors, and 'truthers' who should know better. This one error has me "shouting at the radio" more than any other.

For example, Katherine Watt, whose work I respect, routinely makes the mistake of calling legislation 'Law', so does Sasha Latypova. I have heard James Delingpole, Catherine Austin Fitts, Peggy Hall, Greg Reese, James Roguski, Jane Ruby, Scott Schara, and Maria Zeee all err on this point. Mike Adams makes this error in almost every episode of his Health Ranger Report, and Todd Callender in almost every sentence.

I respect their research, but through this one abuse of language alone, they unwittingly confer on governments a false authority to play God in the lives of others; dictate to us what we must do with our bodies, our property, our children, and even out thoughts; and then have us bend the knee and plead for 'exemptions' that they may grant at their pleasure by a counterfeit mercy.

Lawyers, too, are generally taking government writ as gospel by confining their range of motion to the shrinking legal box of legislation. Even to call them 'lawyers' is a misnomer when, for the most part, they are not dealing in Law at all but in the muck of legislation. They are not lawyers but corporate power-brokers and negotiators cutting deals with corporate entities, wherein you and I are regarded as no more than corporations.

So, if there's only one thing you take away from this book, let it be this...

STOP CALLING LEGISLATION LAW!

This one shift in mindset will produce good fruit. You will see legislation for the toilet fodder it really is, and even 'legislation' may be too generous a term because the entities that forge it, pretend to debate it, and dutifully pass it are all corporations, that is to say, invented things, and their prolixious documents amount to nothing more than corporate policy, binding only upon themselves and their own employees. All governments, parliaments, courts, and police forces *are* corporations, and their policies, procedures, and decrees have no more authority over us than if McDonald's or Starbucks had written them.

It boils down to this: God makes Law, man makes legislation, and corporations make company policy. How dare they ascribe to men and to the institutions of men the authority to make Law? When there is already so little airtime afforded genuine voices for Freedom, we cannot afford to build on such a broken foundation.

Further, Acts and statutes are, in effect, contracts that one party draws up, one party negotiates with itself, and one party signs, and then thinks to impose on another party, us, without our signature or consent, much less our

Informed Consent. Governments and corporations may
not impose any demand on you unless you have
voluntarily, and with full knowledge, signed a contract
that includes your agreement to the demand. Therefore, if
some would-be enforcer tells you, "You have to do this.
This is the law," you say, "Show me the document that
says this, and show me where I signed it."

Still, I wrestled with calling this book, *Know Your Legal
Rights* instead of *Know Your Lawful Rights*. Though the
Lawful is as far above the Legal as the heavens are above
the Earth, we may on occasion operate in the Legal, and
though we are not subject to the pieces of paper written
by men, we may still cite them on a Legal stage to compel
enforcers to obey the contracts binding upon themselves.

If we enter the Legal, therefore, we do so as an actor
puts on a costume to play a role. We do not *live* in the
Legal, any more than an actor would live his entire life
in the costume and lines of his character, but we may
play a role in it sometimes. Imagine the hell of an actor
trapped forever in the fictional time and place of his
theatrical persona with no way out, even worse if he lost
all memory of his prior life outside the role and forgot
there was an exit. That nightmarish condition describes
much of Humanity today, but not you or me. If we ever
operate in the Legal, we remember that we are not *of* the
Legal.

In the end, I went with *Lawful* for the title, because
that is the realm of Truth, whereas Legal is the realm of
fiction. Like a thieving usurper, Legal has crept into the
throne room of our Sovereignty and presumes to rule as

King, but he is an impostor and must be ousted if we are to restore our Birthright in the Lawful.

This requires a shift in mindset. We have much to learn, or rather unlearn, as we dismantle the lies, programming, and conditioning that have kept us from ourselves. The walls of my own perception too must dissolve to write this book. Ironically, COVID did much of that work for me by exposing the evil, and the doers of that evil, that have long crouched in the shadows and quietly infested our institutions. As the poet Theodore Roethke wrote, "In a dark time the eye begins to see." I imagine God's hand on the dimmer switch of our awareness and gradually turning up the light.

And as that dawn returns, Government shall no longer be enthroned in the minds of men, nor shall its ideologies, stupidity, or stupid ideologies. Alas, the evildoers have been assisted in their acts of theft and destruction by a largely compliant population. People seem to have embedded in their consciousness, "I must obey Government," turning it into a religion. Even after the COVID era, with its ample demonstration that Government is a cult seeking our enslavement and death, this idea is still firmly lodged in most people.

For example, I notice when taking flights in the U.S. that I am the only one refusing the body-scan chambers that the Transport and Security Administration (TSA) puts people through, the photos taken after international arrivals, and the biometric scans even at departure gates, all of which are Fourth-Amendment violations and, in the case of the body scans, medical violations too. Seeing the compliance of others is deeply frightening to me because they will passively watch tyranny happen to others and just stand idly by, or perhaps get out their mobile phones to record it and win coveted clicks on social media. At their worst, they will turn in their neighbours, or even other family members, and report non-compliance to the authorities.

I also recently saw a New Zealand honey producer torching his hives and with them, millions of bees, because the government told him to. Before that, an Australian producer allowed government agents on to his property where they drowned his bees in petrol. It is an enraging spectacle. The bees, at least, have enough regard for their own survival to sting their attackers, but many compliant humans have no sting of their own, even when directly assailed.

In Britain, meanwhile, households keeping even a single chicken are "required" to register their bird. To anyone paying even perfunctory attention, it is obvious the government will at some point try to use this information to destroy every last vestige of independent food production by conjuring some disease scare such as 'bird flu' and culling yet more hens.

Why do people keep falling for these deceptions? I want to shake them and say, "Moron, the government is trying to destroy you and your business, and the food supply along with it!" And if the autocrats can't entirely cause starvation, they are doing their best to destroy independent farmers who might produce clean, healthy food. That way, they can force consumption of their highly processed, poison-laced megacorporation stomach fillers sold in supermarkets which, in turn, are extremely vulnerable to supply-line sabotage.

Even the very word, 'Government'—which means 'mind control'—is offensive to me now. Who do these people think they are to 'govern' anyone, let alone to tax us, especially when they operate in, and are promoted by, a system that rewards corruption, laziness, and incompetence, in a culture of failing upwards? As Christ said of the Pharisees in his day, "they bind heavy burdens and grievous to be borne, and lay them on men's shoulders, but do not lift a finger to help them" (*Matthew* 23:4).

In Jesus' day, the Pharisees were a hypocritical religious cult, whitewashed tombs full of dead men's bones as he described them, a brood of vipers who strain out gnats but swallow camels (*Matthew* 23). Similarly, today's Pharisees strain out gnats by punishing speech that offends them while swallowing camels of rape, genocide, and theft. Meanwhile, their religion demands of us extortionate tithes, offerings, sacrifices, and ritual performances as, almost every day, they issue some new decree to control us, some new fine or some new fee, and then expect us dutifully to follow and to obey, to follow and to pay.

In the process, our constitutions and Rights declarations are routinely trampled in the name of virtue-signalling slogans such as 'diversity', 'equity', 'inclusion', 'prevention', 'safety', 'security', 'sustainability', and so on. These are empty words when they come from the mouths of tyrants and, as Homer reminds us in *The Odyssey*, "Empty words are evil" (XI.544).

We must therefore reclaim our inherent authority and remember the obvious and irrefutable truth, as stated in the documentary *Strawman*, that "Government is a creation of Man, and a creation of Man can never be above Man." You and I have authority over every thing that Government is and every thing that Government creates. That's just the authority of logic, but Christians have the even more potent authority from our Lord and Saviour to "overcome all the power of the enemy" (*Luke* 10:19), and in case you haven't realized it, governments *are* the enemy.

So I try never to forget, should I face official, police officer, or judge, that I have authority over them and that I am the one giving *them* 'lawful orders', not the other way round, and that, like their father the devil, these operatives must flee when resisted (*James* 4:7). With this book, I am giving shape to that resistance, assembling not just our constitutional weapons but, for those who "put on the full armour of God" (*Ephesians* 6:13), our spiritual weapons too.

I will admit the enormity of this task feels daunting sometimes, for the subject is vaster than any one author can encompass. I do not pretend to have all the answers, and some of my analysis may yet be naive. Just untangling the history of how we got here would take several volumes, delving back even to Biblical times, but what I can do is present the conceptual frameworks to reclaim our Rights, dispel the illusions that have tried to imprison us, fortify your heart for the battles and skirmishes ahead, and introduce you to solutions and solvers.

I also want to minimize the cost and dangers of the non-compliance we must embrace if we want to get through this. Your instincts are already telling you not to comply, and you may be willing to sacrifice for the cause, but let us be smart about our non-compliance, disciplined, and prepared. Let us also be open to learning more, and honing our skills, as time passes, for these are early days in clawing back our Sovereignty.

The God Stuff

Now, having got Biblical with you a few times by now, I recall that some readers objected to my Scriptural references in *Know Your Medical Rights*. If that is you, season your skepticism a while and acknowledge that even our enemies are deeply religious and that their destructive influence cannot be otherwise explained. For example, do they lie? Then entertain the possibility that they serve the Father of Lies (*John* 8:44). Do they couch their tyranny in virtue-signalling language? Then ask if they serve he who masquerades as an angel of light (*2 Corinthians* 11:14-15). Do they persecute those who tell the truth and who try to warn others? Then consider if they worship he who accuses the righteous (*Revelation* 12:10). And, are they predatory? Then witness how they take after the devil who "prowls around like a roaring lion looking for someone to devour" (*1 Peter* 5:8).

Ask yourself, too, if the assaults against our bodies—not just from venomous injections but from poisons in our food, water, air, sea, and land—are motivated by a hatred of the Most High in whose image we are made (*Genesis* 1:26-27).

Also, do they act in concert across nations, writing the same legislation, telling the same lies, and issuing the same decrees, all at the same time? Then consider how they must be coordinating in secret, making secret oaths and secret pacts, and that secret oaths are the currency of secret societies such as Freemasonry. Have you observed officials, elected or otherwise, along with doctors, judges, and police, desecrating their public oaths, whether to the Constitution or Oath of Office, Hippocratic Oath, or Constable's Oath? Could that mean they are instead cleaving to secret oaths? Would you describe them as psychopaths, meaning they can kill, loot, steal, and destroy others, including children, without remorse? Then is it possible their consciences have been seared (*1 Timothy* 4:1-2) during initiation rites of atrocity? You and I have empathy enough to imagine ourselves in someone else's shoes if they tell us we are causing them harm, but that mechanism has been annihilated in the politicians and bureaucrats of today.

And if you are disposed to excuse the naive ranks of secret-society orders, where the higher-ups—or rather, the lower-downs of an inverted pyramid—conceal the real agenda from initiates, know that even at the First Degree of Freemasonry, they have already condemned themselves by an oath of atrocity. As reported at evangelicaltruth.com, the initiate swears to secrecy "under no less a penalty than that of having my throat cut across, my tongue torn out by its roots, and buried in the rough sands of the sea at low-water mark."

Therefore, show me a Freemason who purports to be a Christian, and I will show you a child of Hell. Christ warned us that no-one can serve two masters, for he will love one and despise the other (*Matthew* 6:24). We infer that the Hell-spawn of today are not just ignoring their public oaths but actively hating them, and that they hate the *Bill of Rights, Magna Carta,* and every other righteous text. Christ also warned that these traitors would plead their good works to him at the Judgment, to which he will reply, "Away from me. I never knew thee!" (*Matthew* 7:22-23).

Meanwhile, you may observe how governments are serving dogmas that try to turn reality upside-down, even going beyond Orwell's "War is peace. Freedom is slavery. Ignorance is strength." In their worldview, good is evil and evil good, love is hate and hate love, health is sickness and sickness health, male is female and female male, truth is lies and lies are truth. Democracy is dictatorship, food is starvation, medicine poison, and justice injustice. Child protection is child trafficking, and to serve and protect is to extort and destroy.

Also, when it comes to climate-change deceptions, hot is cold and cold is hot. If you find this last element jolting, note how the climate-change narrative has followed the same playbook as COVID: take a threat that is negligible or non-existent and inflate it into a harbinger of planetary doom. To bring about such overthrows of reason requires a constant barrage of indoctrination, censorship, propaganda, fear-mongering, and psychological torture, areas where so-called 'intelligence agencies' have long honed their dark arts.

With such intense attack in the arena of ideas, and with ideas being broadcast through the invisible medium of the air, might you infer this is a spiritual battle too? Do you sense a malevolent spiritual entity or network behind the scenes? Might you call that entity Satan or Lucifer? And if such an impostor set up a throne and called himself God or Messiah, would that not be the king of all inversions?

Still, I venture that you and I are so *over* state-sanctioned lies by now that the tyrants have given up trying to persuade us. Yet they must still convince *themselves*, if only to quell any protest from Conscience. "Uncertain way of gain," to quote Shakespeare's *Richard III*, "but I am in/ So far in blood that sin will pluck on sin./ Tear-falling pity dwells not in this eye" (IV.ii).

Meanwhile, if you harbour distrust of Christians, bear in mind that not all who *call* themselves Christians are truly members of the Body of Christ. Some are wolves in sheep's clothing or, calling on Shakespeare again, beautiful tyrants, fiends angelical, dove-feathered ravens, honorable villains, serpent hearts (*Romeo and Juliet*, III.ii). And some are false prophets, eager to share what "God told me."

Beware, too, of 'Controlled Opposition', those tasked with drawing dissidents into a 'Limited Hangout' that refuses to look at deeper and more horrid realities. Keep your wits about you, practise discernment, and sniff out the spiritual rot of these whitewashed tombs full of dead men's bones (*Matthew* 23:27).

But seek out those who genuinely *are* in Christ and who have chosen his ultimate authority over the false authority of men. We Christians may be all that is standing between you and annihilation. Have you noticed how Christian voices have taken the lead in recent years in denouncing and exposing the perpetrators? When, since the days of Moses or Joshua, has there been such a need for a fierce Christian army?

Do not resent your protectors, who are already paying a price for our faith. As Harrison Smith observed in a May 2024 interview with Maria Zeee, Christianity is under attack today because it impedes the totalitarian agenda…

"It makes it hard to control people. It makes it hard to deceive and manipulate. When the whole society is sincerely righteous and desires truth and desires justice, then you can't get away with things very easily. You have to have a whole system that's corrupt and fallen, and then it makes it easy to scam, it makes it easy to get one over. They want the dog-eat-dog world where they can screw somebody over and destroy them and suffer no consequences. So Christianity is a barrier to control, it's a barrier to oppression. **It gives you something higher than earthly authority, and that naturally pisses off the earthly authority**" (emphasis mine).

Speaking of earthly authority, I will not pin my hopes on a political solution to our woes. The *Declaration of Independence* doesn't tell us to "abolish" this or that political party or political candidate, nor does it call on us to favour one traitor, despot, pussy-grabber, or paedophile over another. No, it is our "duty" to abolish any *form* of Government that is destructive of Life, Liberty, and the Pursuit of Happiness.

Many more people are aware now that political parties oppose each other in only the most superficial ways, but when it comes to matters that really affect our lives, they are firm allies in trying to despoil us. As Mike Adams observed, in an April 2024 article,...

> "The Democrats have actively destroyed this once-great nation, but the Republicans were either wholly complicit or stood by and did nothing while the arsonists set fire to the pillars of our constitutional republic. As is now obvious to anyone paying attention, we no longer have a functioning civil society in the United States of America. We have a failed government, failed election integrity, a failed justice system, a failed counterfeit currency, fake corporate media, fake war propaganda, a failed educational system, and a weaponized system of science and medicine that literally develops and deploys biological weapons against the American people."

Why do politicians act in concert against us, no matter what party they're in? Because, deep down, they're not really Democrats or Republicans, Conservatives or Labour, or whatever. These are just convenient labels for their sham political theatre. No, they serve but one party, and that is the party of Freemasonry. According to Bible scholar David Carrico, in a November 2019 episode of *Now You See TV*,...

> "If you look at the Democratic Party and the Republican Party, if you look close enough, both are Masonically controlled... These two American political parties, they are just the expression of two Masonic philosophies that both have the same ultimate goal, and that will be the New World Order."

That's why petitions and protests are useless when you're dealing with them. So too are polls when they have no compunction about rigging elections. As Max Igan observes, "There's nobody you can vote in. There's nobody you can vote out. There's no political remedy to this system."

True, Max. There is no political remedy, but other remedies are at hand. That's why I have written this book, a battle manual for warriors determined to overthrow tyrants of every stripe. One way or another, we must reclaim our Sovereignty, our freedom of action, even our freedom of thought. I do not mean a 'Great Reset' such as our enemies have conceived, but at least a Great Reckoning to restore Justice and consequence for the innumerable Crimes Against Humanity unleashed against Mankind. When, like a mighty river Justice returns, the

overlords will be destroyed as surely as Pharaoh and his
chariots were destroyed when they chased Moses into the
Red Sea (*Exodus* 14:26-28). I trust this book shall serve as
armour and weapon in the battle ahead, for battle it is,
and battle it will be.

Abdiel LeRoy

FROM THE AUTHOR

Thank you for reading my book, and if you found value in it, I would welcome your review wherever you buy books. A few sentences would suffice.

I wrote it in bewildered haste, a reflection of the authoritarian sprint now in motion, but did my best to ensure all is properly sourced and that the Internet links work. If I've missed something you think important, please send me an email at RenewedTestament@protonmail.com.

Please also let me know if you find a broken link. The powers-that-shouldn't-be are replicating Orwell's 'Memory Hole' of *1984* and pulling down inconvenient facts and opinions that do not suit the view they want us to have of the world, or of its history, as they prepare for future holocaust denial. I have noticed this especially on YouTube which, like an industrial polluter, dumps poison into the waterways of public discourse and opinion.

Though I don't always agree with U.S. senator Rand Paul, I concur with his statement that YouTube "are the worst." I have even seen nightmarish clips embedded in the advertising sections of YouTube videos, apparently some kind of Nudge-Unit tactic to disturb our dreams and instill yet more fear. The intent seems to be, "If we can't make you afraid of COVID, we'll make you afraid of us." Though some true voices yet remain on the platform, it has become so infiltrated and surveilled by now that, whenever possible, I listen to these voices, and post videos of my own, on alternative hosting sites such as Bastyon, BitChute, and Brighteon.

Beyond protecting the historical record, it is also crucial we guard our charters, constitutions, and Rights declarations from tampering and trashing. The powers-that-shouldn't-be will surely attempt this ultimate blasphemy, this 'intercision' of our collective soul, this second Crucifixion, but our inalienable Rights are kept in a place no evil can touch.

I've noticed already how the British, Australian, U.S., and Canadian governments are tinkering with the archives, even hurriedly rewriting legislation that contained inconvenient Rights protections. Well, this unlawful conduct has been noted and will be used as evidence against them when, like a mighty river, Justice returns.

But they will not get their dirty, thieving hands on our sacred texts. "Thou shalt keep them, O Lord, thou shalt preserve them from this generation forever" (*Psalm* 12:7). We have guarded them in their pre-2020 form, and this book serves as a document of record as well. I recommend you download the key protective documents I have cited as soon as possible, put them on hard drives, and print them out if you can. As I said, please also notify me if they no longer say what I have faithfully reported. Hold on to your hard-copy dictionaries too, lest the tyrants try to destroy language as Orwell warned us they would.

Now that I have fortified our medical Rights, my next books will champion our lawful Rights and financial Rights. Banks and central banks are becoming increasingly tyrannical, unconstitutional, unreliable, and untrustworthy. One major threat is central-bank digital currencies (CBDC) which, if implemented, will crush individual privacy and allow tyrants to reward your behaviour if they like it and penalize your behaviour and speech if they don't. Meanwhile, the entire banking system is becoming increasingly insolvent, meaning a greater likelihood of bank runs, bank failures, bank freezes, and even bank bail-ins, where they just help themselves to the contents of your account.

To hedge against these, I have begun buying and vaulting goldbacks, a form of currency embedding 24-karat gold, and am now using them to buy and sell, to give and receive, whether face-to-face or on-line. The smallest denomination, a one-goldback note, contains one thousandth of a troy ounce. The other denominations are 5, 10, 25, and 50.

If you want to buy goldbacks, I have an affiliate link at https://Geni.us/Goldbacks. I earn a modest fee on any purchases you make there at no extra cost to you. I became a partner with Goldbacks in 2023 after I was 'demonetized' on Substack and reader donations were refunded without my consent.

The best way to support my work, however, is to buy and review my books of fiction, non-fiction, memoir, poetry, and epic poetry, all listed below. You can avoid Amazon entirely now by buying directly from me at https://payhip.com/poetprophet.

Finally, thank you for embracing this labour of love. May the Most High bless you and keep you, make his face to shine upon you, and give you everlasting life. May he go with you and ahead of you, before you and behind you, a pillar of cloud by day and a pillar of fire by night, and bring you to places he hath prepared.

Much love,
Abdiel LeRoy

BOOKS BY A. LEROY
(ABDIEL LEROY)

NON-FICTION

KNOW YOUR MEDICAL RIGHTS

Did you know that, under international law, no-one can demand you get a medical test, wear a mask, or have any other medical procedure?

And did you also know that no emergency, even if it threatens the life of a nation, takes away any of your rights? Or that any politician or pundit who attempts to persecute a group based on medical status is committing a Crime Against Humanity?!

Meanwhile, international law also confirms YOUR MEDICAL STATUS IS CONFIDENTIAL, a protection supported by medical codes dating back millennia to the Hippocratic Oath.

Yet governments are not only demanding we hand over this sacred information but are still using it to divide and discriminate, penalizing bodily sovereignty and autonomy, and they are poised to inflict even worse atrocities than they did during 'COVID'.

"I know in my heart that these measures are an atrocity," writes Abdiel LeRoy in the Introduction, "and my spirit rebels against them, but just having that instinct is not enough now. WHAT ARE MY RIGHTS?"

Here is your constitutional Bible, a rebuking voice to tyranny, and a rallying cry for all Mankind.

KNOW YOUR LAWFUL RIGHTS

Not since the days of Noah has Earth witnessed such an all-out assault on life and livelihood as we see today. The false authorities are pursuing their agenda of extermination and enslavement with a ruthlessness most of us could never have imagined.

In this sequel to *Know Your Medical Rights*, Abdiel LeRoy dismantles the lies, programming, and conditioning that have kept us from ourselves. He reminds you who you are, a three-dimensional being standing above the two-dimensional fictions of government, and he empowers you to tear down strongholds of dogma and dictatorship.

"I will show you that all is counterfeit, all theatre," LeRoy writes in the Introduction, "and that counterfeit governments, issuing counterfeit currencies and writing counterfeit legislation masquerading as Law, are wielding counterfeit authority. It's so much easier to refuse and refute that authority when you know its enforcers are beneath you and that they are peddling fictional constructs."

Then, having pierced through the illusions and mind-tricks of tyrants, he lays before you the weapons of True Law you will need to regain your Sovereignty and Birthright. This book will serve you as armour and weapon in the battles ahead.

KNOW YOUR FINANCIAL RIGHTS

Your tax compliance has been funding genocide. Your debt payments are rewarding banks who never lent you anything in the first place. Meanwhile, any digits in your bank account can be seized or frozen at a moment's notice.

The entire financial system has been engineered to extort us, enslave us, and then finally to exterminate us when we've nothing left to give. It's time to tear it down and stop funding our demise, and it's time to transact in ways that tyrants can not monitor, surveil, and control.

Know Your Financial Rights is the final installment of a tyrant-slaying trilogy of constitutional bibles, recalling the mission of Bible prophets who overthrew kings.

Wear this book as a garment of protection, wield it as a spiritual sword, and weaponize it against the legion of traitors now conspiring against us.

THE GOURMET GOSPEL COLLECTION
A Better Eden/ It Was for Freedom/ Foes to Grace

Desperate to escape from an eating disorder, Abdiel went on a quest for "the truth that sets me free," and found it in a rediscovery of Grace—the unmerited favor of God—that church teachings rarely, if ever, reveal.

With the help of great writers, Christian thinkers, and of course the Bible itself, he returns to an Eden of the mind that predates the command, 'Do not...', and where sin is neither possible nor perceived.

DUELING THE DRAGON COLLECTION
Five Memoirs About Living and Working in China

A wide-eyed expat is detained by Beijing cops and told to sign a false confession. Will he make it out of China alive? *Dueling the Dragon* is a great adventure story, but *this* one just happens to be true!

With a journalist's eye and lively wit, LeRoy's memoirs expose the deep levels of corruption tearing at China's social fabric.

MY PORTABLE PARADISE
Transform Your Life Through House Sitting

Tired of burning bitter hours in a toxic job? Tired of the same old routine? Tired of the stress and hassle of paying rent, or a mortgage? Then house sitting may be for you.

From a beach house in Costa Rica, this veteran house sitter and author welcomes you to share in the joys and blessings he has received.

Whether you're a 'digital nomad' looking for adventure, retired and seeking a change of scenery, or just looking for a simpler life, you'll find gentle guidance in this book. And... it might just change your life!

POETRY COLLECTIONS

WELL VERSED
To Shakespeare, Poets, and the Performing Arts

Dante is famous. He imagined Hell,
A plain of burning flakes and sulphurous smell,
Pour souls afflicted in a sorry state,
And names the enemies he loves to hate.

But he's no match for Milton's inspiration,
No poet greater in imagination.
Yet Shakespeare most gets ink within these pages.
'Twas he who said, "Our praises are our wages!"

VERSES VERSUS EMPIRE
I—*The Bush Era*

It's Judgment Day, and George W. Bush strides confidently towards the throne of God. How will the Almighty respond? Find out in this work of devastating satire.

From Bush through Obama to Trump, LeRoy charts an epic course through the inferno of U.S. politics, exposing the fraud and folly of empire and its rulers.

VERSES VERSUS EMPIRE
II—*The Obama Era*

As the late historian Howard Zinn said, "There have only been a handful of people who use their wit to take down the pretensions of the high and mighty."

Here is one of them, a resounding voice for our times, an offering of hope and beauty rising from the ashes of a broken political system, a creation of unprecedented literary power. Witness herein that the pen really *is* mightier than the sword!

VERSES VERSUS EMPIRE
III—The Trump Era

The intellectuals of this dangerous age,
However eloquent, however sage,
Indicting empire with insightful prose,
Have not yet healed the nation's woes.

To tear down strongholds of the powers-that-be
Who give lip service to Democracy,
A poet of prophetic voice steps forward
To prove the pen is mightier than the sword!

THE VERSES VERSUS EMPIRE COLLECTION
Poetry and Prose on Three Imperial Presidencies
2001-2021

Through three imperial presidencies
The poet cries, voice in the wilderness,
Reed swaying in the wind,[1] a bruisèd reed,[2]
His motion stirred to music,
Daring to see and state the obvious,
Decry hypocrisy, prophetically to see
Not just the future but the now,
The awful now and make some sense of it,
The world a stage on which plays out
Congressional pantomime, a knot
Unable to untie itself. The blood
Of innocents cries out to Heaven where
These incensed lines as incense burn
With hate of Hate and hope of Hope.

EPIC POETRY
(FICTION IN VERSE)

ELIJAH

*A Fictional Reinvention of the Great Prophet's Life
in an Epic Poem*

*He called down fire and false prophets slew,
He raised the dead, conversed with angels, flew
To Heaven in a chariot of fire
And fled from Jezebel's murderous ire.*

*But there is more, O so much more to tell,
Of meeting Moses and a dragon's spell,
Shapeshifting goddesses at Cherith Brook.
Such wonders will unfold within this book!*

OBAMA'S DREAM
The Journey That Changed the World

This sordid theatre we call politics
Is full of lies and dirty tricks,
But what if angels came into the fray
To challenge presidents and what they say?

And what if one appeared before God's throne
Where wicked schemes of men are overthrown
And Satan tried a victim to condemn?
This book turns upside-down the world of men!

THE EPICS COLLECTION
Obama's Dream, Elijah, Jezebel's Lament

It is an age-old struggle, that between
The earthly power of presidents and kings
Encountering divine power, wonders seen
When prophets pray. This theme the author brings

In reinvention of the Bible tales,
Ascents to Heaven, wondrous revelation,
Shapeshifting goddesses in his portrayals,
Joined by the author's audiobook narrations.

FICTION

JEZEBEL'S LAMENT

A Defense of Reputation, a Denouncement of the prophets Elijah and Elisha

In this companion piece to *Elijah*, Israel's tyrant queen tells her side of the story and why she so detests that "unkempt fire-and-brimstone hairy hermit" who prophesies dogs shall eat her corpse.

"Yes, I had to get rid of some inconvenient men of God along the way, and a stubborn wine producer, but in all this I did only what a queen *must* do in such circumstances to protect herself, to safeguard her family and the royal line."

You will hear of trysts and treason in this witty rendering by Abdiel LeRoy.

THE CHRISTMAS TREE
A Tale of Divine Awakening

A tree is torn from his forest home and all that he loves, but there is courage in the heart of a little boy to protect his belovèd tree.

The author dreamt up this story from witnessing Christmas trees being abandoned on city sidewalks, but here his invention of a magical journey for one such tree will transport you through time and space and otherworldly encounter, even to the throne of God!

THE PRINCE'S OATH
A Tale From Afghanistan

An innocent man must lose his freedom, an innocent girl must yield her virginity, in this traditional tale from an era of kings.

From bandit attacks in a forest to treacherous plots at court, love will undergo many trials with the Almighty's help, even if it comes in the form of a cheeky little mouse!

THE CHRISTIAN REVERIES COLLECTION
The Christmas Tree/ The Prince's Oath/ Obama's Dream

You'll know a tree according to its fruit,
Three golden branches with one holy root,
The Good Book's inspiration running through,
This trinity uplifting hearts anew.

Not 'R'-rated as the Epics Collection,
These tales are more of a 'PG' selection,
But still have magic, shapeshifters, and all
Those elements mythology recalls.

APPENDIXES

APPENDIX I

A HANDY GUIDE TO CONSTITUTIONAL AND RIGHTS PROTECTIONS

Printable version at
Geni.us/HumanRights
(case sensitive)

Here are listed the most egregious categories of government banditry in the COVID era, followed by their constitutional antidotes. Please feel free to inform the author (RenewedTestament@protonmail.com) of additional protections you would like to see added.

Government Is Inferior to the People

International

"Because government is a creation of man, and a creation of man can never be above man, they need your consent before they have the force of law."

— *STRAWMAN* DOCUMENTARY

"We the people created government; they are the fiction. A fiction can never gain authority over its creator."

— JACQUIE PHOENIX

All Emergency Measures

International

"No state party shall, **even in time of emergency threatening the life of the nation**, derogate from the Covenant's guarantees of the right to life; freedom from torture, cruel, inhuman or degrading treatment or punishment, and **from medical or scientific experimentation** without free consent; freedom from slavery or involuntary servitude; the right not to be imprisoned for contractual debt; the right not to be convicted or sentenced to a heavier penalty by virtue of retroactive criminal legislation; the right to recognition as a person before the law; and freedom of thought, conscience and religion. **These rights are not derogable under any conditions even for the asserted purpose of preserving the life of the nation.**"

— SIRACUSA PRINCIPLES (1985),
PARA. 58, APPLYING TO UNITED NATIONS
INTERNATIONAL COVENANT ON CIVIL
AND POLITICAL RIGHTS

United Kingdom

Emergency measures must be scrutinised by Parliament within seven days of being made, and renewed every month.

— CIVIL CONTINGENCIES ACT 2004

"Upholding fundamental human rights."

— CONSTABLE'S OATH (WHICH APPLIES
TO EVERY POLICE OFFICER AT EVERY
RANK)

Injections in Experimental Phase or 'Emergency Use Authorization'

International

"**The voluntary consent of the human subject is absolutely essential.** This means that the person involved should have legal capacity to give consent; should be so situated as to be able to exercise free power of choice, **without the intervention of any element of force, fraud, deceit, duress, overreaching, or other ulterior form of constraint or coercion.**"

— NUREMBERG CODE, PART 1

"It is the duty of physicians who are involved in medical research to protect the life, health, dignity, integrity, **right to self-determination, privacy, and confidentiality of personal information of research subjects**."

— HELSINKI DECLARATION, 1964,
PARA. 9

Injections at Any Time

International

"Any **preventive**, diagnostic and therapeutic medical intervention is only to be carried out with the **prior, free and informed consent** of the person concerned, based on adequate information."

— UNITED NATIONS UNIVERSAL
DECLARATION ON BIOETHICS AND
HUMAN RIGHTS (2005), ARTICLE 6

"The inherent dignity of the human person."

— UNITED NATIONS INTERNATIONAL
COVENANT ON ECONOMIC, SOCIAL AND
CULTURAL RIGHTS (1996), PREAMBLE

"All peoples have the right of self-determination."

— UNITED NATIONS INTERNATIONAL
COVENANT ON ECONOMIC, SOCIAL AND
CULTURAL RIGHTS (1966), PART I,
ARTICLE 1, PARA. 1

"Everyone has the right to life, liberty, and security of person."

— UNITED NATIONS INTERNATIONAL
COVENANT ON CIVIL AND POLITICAL
RIGHTS (1966) ARTICLE 3

Europe

"**The vaccination is NOT mandatory** and that no one is politically, socially, or otherwise pressured to get themselves vaccinated if they do not wish to do so."

— RESOLUTION 2361, PARLIAMENTARY
ASSEMBLY OF THE COUNCIL OF EUROPE,
PARAGRAPH 7.3.1

United Kingdom

"You have the right to accept or refuse treatment that is offered to you, and not to be given any physical examination or treatment unless you have given valid consent."

— NHS CONSTITUTION

"A person must give permission before they receive **any type of medical treatment, test, or examination.**"

— NHS WEBSITE

"Regulations… may not include provision requiring a person to undergo medical treatment. 'Medical treatment' includes vaccination and other prophylactic treatment."

— PUBLIC HEALTH (CONTROL OF DISEASE) ACT 1984, SECTION 45E

United States

"The right of the people to be secure in their persons…."

— FOURTH AMENDMENT

Australia

No **"civil conscription"** in government provision of medical and dental services.

> — AUSTRALIAN CONSTITUTION,
> SECTION 51.23A

Law of the Commonwealth prevails over the law of a State.

> — AUSTRALIAN CONSTITUTION,
> SECTION 109

Canada

Fundamental freedoms include the right to "security of the person."

> — CANADIAN BILL OF RIGHTS (1960),
> PART I, SECTION 1(A)

Interventions by Members of the Public
(closing injection centres and arresting skin-piercers)

United Kingdom

Any man or woman **"may use such force as is reasonable in the circumstances in the prevention of crime,** or in effecting or assisting in the lawful arrest of offenders."

— CRIMINAL LAW ACT (1967), SECTION 3

A person other than a constable may arrest without a warrant anyone who has committed, or is in the act of committing, an indictable offence, including injury to any other person, if "it is not reasonably practicable for a constable to make it instead."

— POLICE AND CRIMINAL EVIDENCE
ACT (1984), SECTION 24A

Police Conduct

United Kingdom

"Upholding fundamental human rights."

— OATH FOR THE OFFICE OF CONSTABLE
(INCLUDED IN SCHEDULE 4 OF THE
POLICE ACT 1996), WHICH APPLIES TO
EVERY POLICE OFFICER AT EVERY RANK.

"You must uphold the law regarding human rights."

— CODE OF ETHICS,
U.K. COLLEGE OF POLICING

"Give and carry out lawful orders only."

— CODE OF ETHICS,
U.K. COLLEGE OF POLICING

Any constable who "exercises the powers and privileges of a constable improperly," or to the detriment of another person, is liable on conviction to **imprisonment for up to 14 years and a fine.**

— CRIMINAL JUSTICE AND COURTS ACT
(2015), SECTION 26

Canada

"Every officer is a peace officer in every part of Canada."

— ROYAL CANADIAN MOUNTED POLICE
ACT (1985), PART I, 11.1 (1)

"Respect the rights of all persons" and "act at all times in a courteous, respectful and honourable manner."

— ROYAL CANADIAN MOUNTED POLICE
ACT (1985), SECTION 37

"I will uphold the Constitution of Canada... and discharge my other duties as Police Constable, faithfully, impartially and according to law."

— CANADIAN POLICE OATH OF OFFICE

Officers shall not "infringe or deny a person's rights or freedoms under the *Canadian Charter*," make any unlawful detention or arrest, "treat any person in a manner that is abusive or unprofessional," or "conduct themselves in a manner that undermines, or is likely to undermine, public trust in policing."

— CANADIAN POLICE CODE OF
CONDUCT

Medical Testing

International

"Any preventive, **diagnostic** and therapeutic medical intervention is only to be carried out with the **prior, free and informed consent** of the person concerned, based on adequate information."

— UNITED NATIONS UNIVERSAL DECLARATION ON BIOETHICS AND HUMAN RIGHTS (2005), ARTICLE 6

Masks

International

"Any **preventive**, diagnostic and therapeutic medical intervention is only to be carried out with the **prior, free and informed consent** of the person concerned, based on adequate information."

— UNITED NATIONS UNIVERSAL DECLARATION ON BIOETHICS AND HUMAN RIGHTS (2005), ARTICLE 6

United Kingdom

"Regulations... may not include provision requiring a person to undergo medical treatment. 'Medical treatment' includes vaccination and other **prophylactic treatment**."

— PUBLIC HEALTH (CONTROL OF DISEASE) ACT (1984), SECTION 45E

Confidentiality and COVID 'Passports'

International

"No one shall be subjected to arbitrary interference with his privacy, family, home, or correspondence."

— UNIVERSAL DECLARATION OF HUMAN RIGHTS, ARTICLE 12

"Nadie será objeto de injerencias arbitrarias en su vida privada, su familia, su domicilio o su correspondencia."

— UNIVERSAL DECLARATION OF HUMAN RIGHTS, ARTICLE 12

"Whatever I see or hear in the life of men which ought not to be spoken of abroad, whether in connection with my professional practice or not, **I will not divulge**, as reckoning that all such should be kept secret."

— HIPPOCRATIC OATH

"The privacy of the persons concerned and the confidentiality of their personal information should be respected."

— UNITED NATIONS UNIVERSAL
DECLARATION ON BIOETHICS AND
HUMAN RIGHTS (2005), ARTICLE 9

"Privacy, and confidentiality of personal information of research subjects."

— HELSINKI DECLARATION, PARA. 9

United Kingdom

"A duty of confidence" and "consent for the disclosure and use of their personal information." Patients may deny sharing of personal information between healthcare professionals.

— NHS CODE OF PRACTICE (2003)

United States

"The right of the people to be secure in their persons, houses, papers, and effects, against unreasonable searches and seizures, shall not be violated, and no Warrants shall issue, but upon probable cause, supported by Oath or affirmation, and particularly describing the place to be searched, and the persons or things to be seized."

— BILL OF RIGHTS, FOURTH
AMENDMENT

Medical Discrimination

International

"Persecution against any identifiable group" listed among 'Crimes against humanity'.

— ROME STATUTE OF THE
INTERNATIONAL CRIMINAL COURT
(1998), ARTICLE 7

"Everyone is entitled to all the rights and freedoms set forth in this Declaration, **without distinction of any kind**", including opinion or other status.

— UNITED NATIONS UNIVERSAL
DECLARATION OF HUMAN RIGHTS,
ARTICLE 2

"All are entitled to equal protection against any discrimination."

— UNITED NATIONS UNIVERSAL
DECLARATION OF HUMAN RIGHTS,
ARTICLE 7

Europe

"Ensure that no one is discriminated against for not having been vaccinated due to possible health risks **or not wanting to be vaccinated**."

— RESOLUTION 2361, PARLIAMENTARY
ASSEMBLY OF THE COUNCIL OF EUROPE,
PARAGRAPH 7.3.2

No discrimination on any ground, including "discrimination based on disability, **medical conditions** or genetic features."

— EUROPEAN CONVENTION ON HUMAN
RIGHTS, ARTICLE 14, AND EUROPEAN
COURT GUIDANCE ON ARTICLE 14
(PARA. 164)

Violation when an employee is fired for having an infection.

— GUIDANCE ON ARTICLE 14, CITING
EUROPEAN COURT CASE PRECEDENT,
I.B. V. GREECE, 2013 (PARA. 208)

United Kingdom

No discrimination on any ground, including "discrimination based on disability, **medical conditions** or genetic features."

— HUMAN RIGHTS ACT (1998), WHICH
INCLUDES EUROPEAN CONVENTION ON
HUMAN RIGHTS (ARTICLE 14) AND
EUROPEAN COURT GUIDANCE
(PARA. 164)

No discrimination on any ground, including **other status.**

> — HUMAN RIGHTS ACT (1998),
> ARTICLE 14

No discrimination on the basis of religion or belief.

> — EQUALITY ACT (2010)

Police required to "eliminate discrimination, harassment, victimisation and any other conduct that is prohibited by or under the Equality Act 2010."

> — PUBLIC SECTOR EQUALITY DUTY
> (2011)

"Take **a proactive approach** to opposing discrimination."

> — POLICE CODE OF ETHICS, COLLEGE OF
> POLICING

Lockdowns, Curfews, Quarantines, etc.

International

"No free man shall be seized or imprisoned, or stripped of his rights or possessions, or outlawed or exiled, or in any way destroyed, nor will we proceed with force against him, or send others to do so, except by the lawful judgment of his peers or by the law of the land [Common Law]." Therefore, **quarantine measures can only be applied on an individual basis and by trial by jury.**

— MAGNA CARTA, ARTICLE 39

"Right to freedom of association with others."

— UNITED NATIONS INTERNATIONAL COVENANT ON CIVIL AND POLITICAL RIGHTS, ARTICLE 22, PARA. 1

United States

No person shall be "deprived of life, liberty, or property, without due process of law."

— BILL OF RIGHTS, FIFTH AMENDMENT

Canada

Fundamental freedoms include "the right of the individual to life, liberty, security of the person and enjoyment of property, and the right not to be deprived thereof except by due process of law."

— CANADIAN BILL OF RIGHTS (1960),
PART I, SECTION 1(A)

Legislation shall not "authorize or effect the arbitrary detention, imprisonment or exile of any person."

— CANADIAN BILL OF RIGHTS, 1960,
PART I, SECTION 2(A)

Right to Assembly

International

"Right of peaceful assembly."

— UNITED NATIONS INTERNATIONAL
COVENANT ON CIVIL AND POLITICAL
RIGHTS, ARTICLE 21

United Kingdom

"Everyone has the right to freedom of peaceful assembly and to freedom of association with others."

— HUMAN RIGHTS ACT, ARTICLE 11

United States

"The right of the people peaceably to assemble, and to petition the Government for a redress of grievances."

— BILL OF RIGHTS, FIRST AMENDMENT

Right to Travel

International

Anyone may **"leave and return to our kingdom unharmed and without fear."**

— MAGNA CARTA, ARTICLE 42

Everyone has freedom of movement both within a state and to leave any country and return to it. Everyone has the Right to seek and enjoy political asylum, to change one's nationality, and none may be arbitrarily deprived of nationality.

— UNITED NATIONS UNIVERSAL
DECLARATION OF HUMAN RIGHTS,
ARTICLES 13 THROUGH 15

United Kingdom

"That all the Subjects of the United Kingdom of Great Britain shall from and after the Union have **full Freedom and Intercourse of Trade and Navigation to and from any port or place** within the said United Kingdom."

— UNION WITH ENGLAND ACT (1707),
SECTION IV

United States

"The ancient roots of the right to travel freely."

— U.S. SUPREME COURT CASE,
KENT V. DULLES, 1958

Canada

Every citizen has the Right to enter, remain in, or leave Canada; to move to, take up residence in, and gain a livelihood in any province.

— CANADIAN CHARTER OF RIGHTS AND
FREEDOMS, SECTION 6

Right to Work

International

"Everyone has the right to work."

— UNITED NATIONS UNIVERSAL
DECLARATION OF HUMAN RIGHTS,
ARTICLE 23

"In no case may a people be deprived of its own means of subsistence."

— UNITED NATIONS INTERNATIONAL
COVENANT ON ECONOMIC, SOCIAL AND
CULTURAL RIGHTS, PART I, ARTICLE 1,
PARA. 2

Work must be freely chosen.

— UNITED NATIONS INTERNATIONAL
COVENANT ON ECONOMIC, SOCIAL AND
CULTURAL RIGHTS, PART III, ARTICLE 6,
PARA. 1

Work must come with "just and favourable conditions."

— UNITED NATIONS INTERNATIONAL
COVENANT ON ECONOMIC, SOCIAL AND
CULTURAL RIGHTS, PART III, ARTICLE 7

Right to Education

International

"Right of everyone to education."

— UNITED NATIONS INTERNATIONAL
COVENANT ON ECONOMIC, SOCIAL AND
CULTURAL RIGHTS, ARTICLE 13, PARA. 1

Right to Cultural Life

International

Right to "take part in cultural life."

— UNITED NATIONS INTERNATIONAL
COVENANT ON ECONOMIC, SOCIAL AND
CULTURAL RIGHTS, ARTICLE 15, PARA. 1

APPENDIX II

THE 'MEDICAL-FREEDOM MOVEMENT' COULD GET US ALL KILLED!

To you leaders of the so-called 'Medical-Freedom Movement'. Whose side are you on, really? Your lazy thinking and wilful ignorance have cost untold numbers of lives. You repeat the same old strategies and tired old phrases that merely trim the weeds of medical tyranny while allowing its poisonous root to spread. Your errors could get us all killed.

Your most dangerous mistake is to base opposition to forced medicine not on the solid ground that it is eternally unlawful, but on the shifting sands of data and statistics. You say something to the effect of, "This disease, or that variant, is too mild to warrant this or that measure." Or, "You shouldn't have a mandate when there is possible risk."

You utter, utter fools! What you are saying is that you'd be absolutely fine with forced medicine if the circumstances were different, such as a more serious disease, or if a safer countermeasure were produced.

Your stupidity is breathtaking. If Rights are expendable depending on conditions on the ground, or depending on statistics that so-called experts tell you, then they're not rights at all; they're flimsy conveniences.

So fuck the 'Science', and uphold our Rights! Forced medicine is eternally unlawful yesterday, today, and forever. And no emergency, whether real or perceived or invented, removes one single medical Right or any other type of Right.

Even if there were a plague on the scale of the Black Death that wiped out half the population, and even if there were some medical intervention proven to be 100% safe and 100% effective, no-one ever, under any circumstances, would have authority to impose it.

And here's your second biggest mistake: that you never defend medical confidentiality. The **Hippocratic Oath** doesn't just say, "First, do no harm" and, "I will administer no deadly medicine," it also says, "I will not divulge." And that principle of Confidentiality is enshrined in international Rights declarations and the **Fourth Amendment** to *The Constitution of the United States of America*.

Yet you're absolutely fine with the government, or an employer, or a travel company knowing your medical status or your vaccination status. It's none of their goddamn business. No-one has to divulge their medical status, and if you're not divulging your medical status, no-one can discriminate against you or persecute you on the basis of it.

Also, if they don't know your medical status, there's no need to apply for a so-called exemption. The word "No" is exemption enough. It always has been, and always will be, exemption enough.

I'm telling you to be a **CONSTITUTIONAL EXTREMIST**. Anything less, and you're dead!

Here's your third mistake. You are forgetting to tell people that, as enshrined in the *Universal Declaration on Bioethics and Human Rights*, along with many more medical codes, we have the Right to **refuse diagnostic measures**, including tests, not just purportedly preventive measures such as masks, injections, quarantines, and lockdowns.

If you had told people that before they went into the charnel houses that hospitals have become, how many more could have been saved? Armed with this information, patients would refuse the supposed 'COVID' tests that have been channeling them into corridors of death and the hospital protocols designed to kill.

But you didn't tell them that, did you? And you're still not telling them. How many lives have been lost through your complicit silence?

Fourth mistake: Lawyers staying inside your little legislative boxes, whinging that you can't go after Big Pharma or doctors or politicians or bureaucrats because they have 'legal immunity'. Do you not realize that all the Acts and statutes that confer this supposed 'legal immunity' are nothing more than corporate contracts that only one party has agreed to and only one party has signed?!

You and I, we the People, were never consulted about these contracts, did not write these contracts, did not negotiate these contracts, didn't even read these contracts, and we certainly didn't sign these contracts. Without our signature, these corporate contracts are not worth the air they're written on. Yet you lawyers are taking them as gospel.

And why, lawyers, instead of drawing on universal and international constitutions, declarations, and conventions, are you confining yourselves within the walls of a shrinking domestic legislative box that provides cover for atrocity and injustice, while you echo the oppressors by mislabeling their tyrannical codes 'law'?

Fifth mistake. Expecting any salvation from a political party or a political candidate, such as Florida governor, Ron DeSantis, just because he throws you a few bones, while you overlook the state statutes he has signed that glaringly promote medical tyranny, including forced quarantine and forced vaccination (SB 2006 and SB 7014), or that desecrate the **First Amendment** (HB 269 and HB 741)?

Remember the duty conferred on us by the *Declaration of Independence*. It doesn't tell us to abolish a political party or a political candidate. It tells us to abolish any *form* of Government that is destructive of Life, Liberty, and the Pursuit of Happiness. And that includes a form of Government that offers a political duopoly where both sides are united in trying to destroy us.

Sixth mistake. You lean disproportionately on the Nuremberg Code, which applies to experimental medicine, while overlooking other international Rights protections and medical codes that apply to all medicine, whether experimental or not. They include the *Universal Declaration on Bioethics and Human Rights*, the *Siracusa Principles*, the **NHS** *Code of Practice*, and the **NHS Constitution**. Where are you going to go when the authorities, the powers-that-shouldn't-be, say, "It's no longer experimental because we've fully approved it. So Nuremberg doesn't apply any more." Where are you going to go?

Finally, you're using the enemy's definitions of words, such as what 'pandemic' means or what 'vaccine' means.

Here's an example that includes the most egregious mistakes. In January 2023, Children's Health Defense (CHD) rejoiced that the New York State Supreme Court ruled against the state's vaccine mandate for healthcare workers. So far, so good, but...

The judge didn't overturn the mandate because it was inherently unlawful, which it is; he did it because it came from an executive order and was not voted on by the legislature. Meaning what? That if the governor can't be sole tyrant, the legislature can? Does an unlawful mandate become valid if only it follows the prescribed procedure?

The court also decided that the mandate was "arbitrary and capricious" on the basis that the "vaccines" do not stop transmission of the "virus"! Meaning what? That if another medical product is conjured that they say *does* stop transmission, you'd be fine with forcing it on people?

CHD's lawyer said that if the mandate "can't stop the spread of COVID, then it's just arbitrary and irrational." Meaning what? That if a product *could* stop the spread of a disease, then forcing it suddenly *would* become rational? Is this what they taught you in law school?

Oh, and she talked about the mandate causing a staffing shortage in New York hospitals. Why are you making all these peripheral arguments that don't address the core tyranny? You are leaving the door open for future tyranny!

Afterwards, CHD president Mary Holland said, "We are thrilled by this critical win against a COVID vaccine mandate, correctly finding that any such mandate at this stage, given current knowledge, is arbitrary."

"At this stage?" "Given current knowledge"? What is she thinking? No! The mandate is arbitrary, period, end of story, eternally, in every circumstance, at every stage, and whatever the current levels of knowledge or ignorance!

Holland's statement echoes another hollow slogan we've heard in 'medical-freedom' circles. "Where there is risk, there must be choice." Again, you're conferring on medical tyrants a false authority to remove choice when they claim there is no risk.

The Children's Health Defense lawyer also complained that the mandate didn't have a religious exemption. So you'd be fine with forcing it on people who don't claim to follow a religion?

My friends. This is a hollow, hollow victory, because you didn't address the core desecrations at work. Again, I say, be a **CONSTITUTIONAL EXTREMIST**. You cannot mandate medicine of any kind, at any time, or in any circumstances.

So before you get more people killed, understand and uphold...

1. All medical coercion is outlawed eternally, whatever the circumstances.
2. Medical confidentiality is eternally sacred.
3. The word "No" is exemption enough.
4. Refuse the tests!
5. Bring Justice, regardless of Acts and statutes, and stop bending the knee to unlawful legislation.

Without all these, all you're doing is nibbling around the edges of medical tyranny but never striking at the root. And that, as I've said, could get us all killed!

Abdiel LeRoy

APPENDIX III

TO BROTHERS AND SISTERS IN 'HEALTHCARE'

Dear brother or sister in healthcare –

We, the people of the United Kingdom, are aware you may experience growing tension between the millennia-old codes of medicine we have inherited and the orders you are asked to carry out.

This tension mirrors the growing discrepancy between international Rights declarations and constitutions, versus Acts and statutes passed by parliaments or regulations decreed by politicians, officials, or institutions. There is also growing divergence between **Common Law**, by which we are all sovereign, and legislation, which is decided by politicians and other tyrants.

But the *Hippocratic Oath* leaves no doubt which applies whenever there is a discrepancy. The Oath also has close kinship with the original 'Royal Law' to love others as we love ourselves. By a small act of imagination, we may put ourselves in the shoes of someone across from us and love them as we would a brother, sister, mother, father, daughter, or son.

The fundamental Rights we all treasure are set down in long-standing declarations such as *Magna Carta* (1215) and the *Universal Declaration of Human Rights* (1948). Furthermore, as the United Nations' *Siracusa Principles* (1984) point out, Rights remain steadfast **"even in time of emergency threatening the life of the nation."**

These and many more international conventions, along with bedrock medical codes such as the *Nuremberg Code*, the **NHS Constitution**, and the **NHS Code of Practice**, ensure that a person's medical status is confidential, shared only with a chosen and trusted physician. Healthcare workers have to get a person's consent even to share such information with a colleague. Much less is medical status grounds for discrimination, persecution, or enforcement of any kind.

Furthermore, the *Universal Declaration on Bioethics and Human Rights* (2005), to which all nations and jurisdictions are bound, states that "any preventive, diagnostic and therapeutic medical intervention is only to be carried out with the prior, free and **informed consent** of the person concerned, based on adequate information." This means no-one can be coerced or compelled to wear a mask or receive an injection ("preventive") or to take a medical test ("diagnostic") without their consent. So-called leaders may not like this, but as your heart and mind will tell you, it is the Truth.

We recall that our nation once stood as a bastion of liberty when tyranny swept across continental Europe. And that, in the wake of this dark episode, the defence pleas of "I was just following orders" proved useless when Justice returned.

If you wish to avoid your own destruction, you will always choose Rights over regulations and love over fear, and if you ever witness medical coercion of any kind, you will uphold your sworn duty to fight it.

A Concerned Man or Woman.

[Download one-page PDF letter at Geni.us/Healthcare.]

APPENDIX IV

TO ARBITERS OF 'RELIGIOUS EXEMPTION'

I would not want to be in your position today. You have been charged with deciding the standing of another soul in the eyes of God, something no-one can determine for another.

The Bible says this directly: "Say not in thine heart, 'Who shall ascend into heaven?' Nor, 'Who shall descend into the deep?" (*Romans* 10:6-7).

Yet it seems you are presuming to do just that, not only making judgments that are God's to make, but threatening the livelihoods of men and women made in God's image on the basis of your own human understanding.

However, I don't need to rely on Scripture to denounce the folly and hubris of these proceedings. International Rights declarations and millennia-old medical codes will do...

The **Hippocratic Oath** does not merely say, "First, do

no harm." It also says, "I will not divulge." In other words, it upholds **Medical Confidentiality**. That means you should not even *know* the medical status of the person before you, much less make any judgment on the basis of it. Confidentiality is also the key protection of the **Fourth Amendment** of the *Bill of Rights*, our "right to be secure in our persons, houses, papers, and effects."

But the criminality of this proceeding does not stop there. Under the *Universal Declaration of Bioethics and Human Rights* (2005), "Any preventive, diagnostic and therapeutic medical intervention is only to be carried out with the prior, free and informed consent of the person concerned." Threatening to destroy a person's livelihood is not consent but naked coercion. Much less is it *informed* consent, especially when an experimental product is proposed, itself a violation of the *Nuremberg Code* (1947) and the *Helsinki Declaration* (1964).

Furthermore, under the *Rome Statute* of the International Criminal Court (1988), persecution against any identifiable group is considered a Crime Against Humanity, as is causing mental distress against a targeted group.

Therefore, consider carefully the sacrilegious basis of these proceedings, and do not presume to rule against anyone put in the contemptible position of having to request from you something that was, is, and always will be their inalienable Right, and that was never yours to withhold or bestow in the first place. As you well know, the word "NO" is, was, and ever will be exemption enough.

Perhaps you are sitting on this panel because you are deemed to have religious expertise, but no religious expertise can presume to play God. That is blasphemy.

Therefore, if you deny religious or other exemption to any nurse or other practitioner who comes before you, prosecution will proceed against you individually by name. As for the consequences for your soul at Judgment, I can only imagine.

[Download one-page PDF letter at Geni.us/Exemption.]

APPENDIX V

TO BROTHERS AND SISTERS IN POLICING

To you, brother or sister in 'law enforcement' –

We, the people of the United Kingdom, are aware you may experience growing tension between your **Oath** and the orders you are asked to carry out.

This tension mirrors the growing discrepancy between international Rights declarations and constitutions, versus acts and statutes passed by parliaments, or regulations decreed by politicians, officials, or institutions. There is also growing divergence between **Common Law**, under which we are all sovereign, and legislation, which is imposed by politicians and other tyrants.

But your **Oath** leaves no doubt you are sworn to uphold **"fundamental human rights."** These are all rooted in the original 'Royal Law' to love others as we love ourselves. By a small act of imagination, we may put ourselves in the shoes of another and love them as we would a brother, sister, mother, father, daughter or son.

The fundamental Rights we all treasure are inalienable and are set down in long-standing declarations such as *Magna Carta* (1215) and the *Universal Declaration of Human Rights* (1948). Furthermore, as the United Nations' *Siracusa Principles* (1984) point out, Rights remain steadfast **"even in time of emergency threatening the life of the nation."**

These and many more international protections, along with bedrock medical codes such as the *Nuremberg Code* and the **NHS** *Constitution*, ensure that medical status is confidential, shared only with a chosen and trusted physician. Much less is medical status grounds for discrimination, persecution, or enforcement of any kind. On the contrary, your own *Code of Ethics* from the College of Policing demands you "take **a proactive approach to opposing discrimination.**"

Furthermore, the *Universal Declaration on Bioethics and Human Rights* (2005), to which all nations and jurisdictions are bound, states that "any preventive, diagnostic and therapeutic medical intervention is only to be carried out with the prior, free and **informed consent** of the person concerned, based on adequate information." This means no-one may be coerced or compelled to quarantine, wear a mask, or receive an injection ("preventive") or to take a medical test ("diagnostic") without their consent. So-called leaders may not like this, but it is the truth.

We recall that our nation once stood as a bastion of

liberty when tyranny swept across continental Europe. And that, in the wake of this dark episode, the defence plea of "I was just following orders" proved useless when Justice returned.

If you wish to avoid your own destruction, you will always choose Rights over regulations and love over fear, and if you ever witness medical coercion of any kind, you will uphold your sworn duty to fight it.

A Concerned Man or Woman.

[Download one-page PDF letter at Geni.us/Police]

APPENDIX VI

LETTER TO U.K. 'MINISTRY OF JUSTICE' REGARDING PROPOSED DESECRATION OF U.K. HUMAN RIGHTS ACT

'Ministry of Justice'
HRAReform@justice.gov.uk

To the British 'Ministry of Justice' —

When Rights protections are regarded as inconvenient by governments, it is clear a tyrannical agenda has taken hold of your hearts.

But I am here to tell you that you and your agenda will be overthrown. This is decreed in Heaven and now unassailable on Earth. We have long seen through your self-righteous façade and your hollow protestations about the good of society, knowing full well that your only intent was ever to harm and destroy.

We are also well aware that all your so-called 'Consultation Documents' are no more than a smokescreen. The intention was never to 'consult' but to confirm under a phoney veneer of consent. Well, neither I nor the British people consent, and without our consent, your decrees are not worth the air they're written on.

I realize that no argument, no matter how true, reasonable or even irrefutable, will normally dissuade you from your malicious intent. So why am I even bothering to write? Because there may be some among you who yet have a shred of decency left, and if not decency, then some shred of conscience, and if not conscience, then fear about the Crimes-Against-Humanity prosecutions that will come your way, and if not fear about prosecution, then fear of the various non-judicial acts of violence stored up for you, and if not fear of what men can do, then fear of God, which I now instill in your hearts.

Even now, the blood of murdered Mankind cries out against you, and your soul will stand naked and trembling before God and Man when Justice returns, as it inevitably will.

There is still time for you to repent of your abominations. If you do not, you shall find the empty words you have drafted will avail you nothing. You shall go to your appointed place, where there is never a moment's joy, despised of God and Mankind, you will go to your doom. This too is decreed in Heaven and now effected on Earth. As for the consequences for your soul at Judgment, I can only imagine.

[Email sent to U.K. 'Ministry of Justice',
HRAReform@justice.gov.uk.
Download one-page letter at Geni.us/JusticeLetter.]

APPENDIX VII

DECLARATION TO RIOT POLICE

Well, look at you all in your battle gear, hiding behind your shields and masks. Are you officers of the 'Law'? The Law is to love others as you love yourself.

Will you honour your oath to the people, to uphold eternal Rights? Or will you be cowards and serve the politicians, those kiddie-fuckers in Government, those criminals who are less than farts in the wind, here today, gone tomorrow?

The Nazis said they were just following orders, then they were put to death. Will you uphold your oath because you care about your soul? Or because you don't want to swing from a noose?

I am the Law, and have authority over you, and if you take one action against us, I will not hesitate to bring death to your door and to your house. And you will go to your eternal destruction, despised of God and Mankind, you will go to your doom. We are watching. God is watching. This is *your* final warning.

Amen, Amen, Amen.

[Download one-page PDF declaration at Geni.us/RiotPolice]

APPENDIX VIII
OTHER RESOURCES

Constitutional Allies

International

Family Guardian Fellowship
https://famguardian.org

Common Law Courts
https://commonlawcourt.com

InPower Movement
https://www.inpowermovement.org

United Kingdom

Big Brother Watch
Website: https://bigbrotherwatch.org.uk/campaigns/
stopvaccinepassports/
Tel.: 24h media line: 07730 439257
Email: info@bigbrotherwatch.org.uk

The White Rose
Website: https://thewhiterose.uk/downloads/

White Rabbit Trust
Website: https://www.youandyourcash.com

Peace Keepers
Website: https://peacekeepers.org.uk.org

Probity Lawful Tax Resistance
Website: https://www.probityco.com

Do Not Consent
Website: https://www.donotconsent.co.uk

Save Our Rights
Website: https://saveourrights.uk

Laworfiction.com
Email: laworfiction@gmail.com

UK Medical Freedom Alliance
Website: http://www.ukmedfreedom.org

Workers of England Union
Website: https://www.workersofengland.co.uk/
Tel.: 0161 883 2552
Email: admin@workersofengland.co.uk

pjhlaw
Website: https://pjhlaw.co.uk/coronavirus-dossiers
Tel.: 01780 757589

Resistance GB
https://www.resistancegb.org

FreeMan-On-The-Land
FMOTL.com

WhatDoTheyKnow.com
whatdotheyknow.com

United States

The Healthy American (Peggy Hall)
https://www.thehealthyamerican.org

Disabled Rights Advocates
Website: https://dradvocates.com

Vaxx Choice
Website: https://vaxxchoice.com

Truth for Health Foundation
Website: https://www.truthforhealth.org
Tel.: 520-777-7092
Fax: 520-797-2948
Email: Info@TruthForHealth.org

Millions Against Medical Mandates
https://mamm.org

Public Health and Medical Professionals for Transparency
https://phmpt.org

InPower Movement
https://www.inpowermovement.org

The Renegade Nation
https://therenegadenation.org

Universal Community Trust
https://www.universal-community-trust.org

Canada

A Warrior Calls
https://awarriorcalls.com

Stand4Thee
https://stand4thee.com

Canadian Covid Care Alliance
canadiancovidcarealliance.org

Australia

AJ Roberts Forum
Website: http://www.mrajroberts.com/community/

Travel

International

Freedom Travel Alliance
Website: https://www.freedomtravelalliance.com/
Email: hello@freedomtravelalliance.com

Injection Injuries

International

Real Not Rare
RealNotRare.com

COVID-19 Vaccine Reactions
https://covidvaccinereactions.com

React19
https://www.react19.org

My Cycle Story
An independent research study collecting data about changes in menstrual cycles
https://mycyclestory.com

German New Medicine
Five Biological Laws that overthrow medical slavery
https://learninggnm.com/SBS/documents/five_laws.html

Cardiovascular Docu-Class
https://stopcardiovasculardisease.com

United States

My Free Doctor.com
https://myfreedoctor.com

Lawyer Referrals

United Kingdom

Lawyers for Liberty
Website: https://lawyersforliberty.uk/, Resources tab

Liberty
Website: https://www.libertyhumanrights.org.uk/advice-and-information/
Advice Line tel.: 0800 988 8177

United States

Concerned Lawyers Network
Website: https://concernedlawyersnetwork.net/resourcestemplates

Law Firms

United Kingdom

Forbes Solicitors
Website: www.forbessolicitors.co.uk
Tel.: 0800 689 3206
Education department: Lucy Harris—01254 222443

The following solicitors have offered 24/7 support in London:

Commons
Tel.: 020 3865 5403

ITN Solicitors
Tel.: 020 3909 8100

Hodge Jones Allen (HJA)
Tel.: 0844 848 0222

Bindmans
Tel.: 020 7305 5638

United States

Liberty Counsel
Website: lc.org

Legal Aid

United Kingdom

Civil Legal Advice
Tel.: 0345 345 4 345

Protest Support

United Kingdom

Green & Black Cross (GBC)

Volunteers operating a Protest Support Line for when you witness an arrest, want support, or have legal questions.
Tel. 07946 541 511
Email courtsupport@protonmail.com

Discrimination

United Kingdom

Equality Advisory Support Service (EASS)
Advice and explanation of Rights under the Equality Act.
Website: https://www.equalityadvisoryservice.com
Tel.: 0808 800 0082
Email: https://www.equalityadvisoryservice.com/app/ask

Employment

United Kingdom

The Legal Cafe
www.legalcafe.co.uk

The Federal Trust for Education and Research
+44 (0)24 7765 1102 info@fedtrust.co.uk

APPENDIX IX
REPAIRING INJECTION DAMAGE

Following are some supplements and therapies said to counter the harmful effects of COVID injections and of other toxins now proliferating. Not medical advice, obviously, but included in case helpful.

Venom/ Spike-Protein Neutralization

EDTA (ethylene diamine tetra acetic acid)
Nicotine (start with minimal dose, 2 mg tablets or patch)
N-Acetyl Cysteine (NAC, 4 x 500 mg/day)
Selenium (200 ug/day, to produce glutathione)
Melatonin
Bromelain (500 mg, twice a day)
Nattokinase (100 mg, twice a day)
Liquorice root extract
Curcumin (nano curcumin, 500 mg, twice a day)

More Spike-Protein Neutralizers

Vitamin C
Hydroxychloroquine
Hyssop
Serrapeptase
Quercetin
Resveratrol
Dandelion leaf extract
Aloe
Prunella vulgaris
Pine-needle tea
Emodin
Neem
Fennel tea
Star anise tea
St. John's wort
Comfrey leaf

Removing Graphene, Nanotech, Heavy Metals

C60 (present in shungite), including 'carbon nano-onions'
Activated charcoal
Humic acid
Clays: Bentonite, Diatomaceous
Tulsi (Ocimum Sanctum) infusion, plant grown at home
Houttuynia cordata infusion, plant grown at home

Aluminium Removal

Orthosilicic acid (OSA)

Cell Health

Alphalipoic acid
Coq10

Other Antioxidants

Astaxanthin
Vitamin D3
Zinc

Myelin Sheath Repair

Omega-3 fatty acids (3000 mg/day)
Ahiflower oil
Goat's milk

Heart Health

Dandelion root tincture

Liver Support

Milk thistle
Desmodium

Kidney Support

Horsetail (evening)
Nettle (evening)

Radiation Mitigation

Melatonin (evening)
Shungite items

Diagnostics

Serum troponin level
D-dimer level
Dark-field blood microscopy
Infrared thermography

Therapies

Intravenous Vitamic C
Hyperbaric oxygen
Ozone therapy
Infrared sauna
Baths with Epsom salts or 1 cup of regular Chlorox
Hydrogen-peroxide nebulization

NOTES

Introduction

1. Addressing the Belmarsh Tribunal that examined state crimes against Julian Assange, Oct. 22, 2021.
2. *Matthew* 17:20.
3. Shakespeare, *Hamlet*, III.ii.
4. At the time of going to press, the first novel in this series, titled *The Lamp of Darkness*, was free in eBook version at various on-line retailers.

Bridging Political Divides

1. Speaking on *Democracy Now!*, Aug. 10, 2018.

II. Our Constitutional Foundation

1. *Hebrews* 12:1.

Constitutions Overrule Legislation

1. Robert Graves, *Wife to Mr. Milton*.

Common-Law Policing

1. I was only able to find a consultation draft of this document, the completed versions having been scrubbed from the RCMP website. Then the draft disappeared too!

Medical Discrimination

1. The Guidestones were destroyed on July 6, 2022 in a mysterious act of sabotage.

Medical Incarceration

1. *Genesis* 25:29-34.

V. The Era of False Prophets

1. *Revelation* 12:12.

The Father of Lies

1. In most categories, the U.K. was the largest contributor of adverse-events data in Pfizer's *Cumulative Analysis* document. This may reflect the U.K.'s earlier date of temporary authorisation for Pfizer's COVID injection, on Dec. 1, 2020, compared with its emergency-use authorization of Dec. 11, 2020 in the U.S.
2. This calculation is derived from the following text in Pfizer's document: "Pregnancy outcomes for the 270 pregnancies were reported as spontaneous abortion (23), outcome pending (5), premature birth with neonatal death, spontaneous abortion with intrauterine death (2 each), spontaneous abortion with neonatal death, and normal outcome (1 each). No outcome was provided for 238 pregnancies (note that 2 different outcomes were reported for each twin, and both were counted)."

Prince of the Air(waves)

1. Attributed to *Telegraph* journalist, Allison Pearson.

The Rise and Fall of Idolatry

1. Blog entry, Jan. 7, 2021.

The Time of True Prophets

1. *Grace Abounding to the Chief of Sinners*, pp.105-106.

Conclusion

1. Shakespeare, *Measure for Measure*, II.ii.
2. *The Odyssey*, Book XI. 544.
3. During interview with Karen Kingston, February 2022.
4. Aleksandr Solzhenitsyn, *Live Not by Lies*.

Poetry Collections

1. Matthew 11:7.
2. Matthew 12:20.

Made in the USA
Coppell, TX
21 September 2025